CAPITALISM
on the Couch

CAPITALISM
on the Couch

Does Our System Need Therapy?

———————

Glen F. Pastores *PsyD, LMFT*

CONSCIOUS
CAPITALISM
PRESS™

Conscious Capitalism Press
www.consciouscapitalism.org/press

Round Table Companies
Packaging, production, and distribution services
www.roundtablecompanies.com
Deerfield, IL

Printed in the United States of America

First Edition: June 2021
10 9 8 7 6 5 4 3 2 1

Library of Congress Cataloging-in-Publication Data
Capitalism on the couch: does our system need therapy?
/ Glen F. Pastores.—1st ed. p. cm.
ISBN Paperback: 978-1-950466-23-8
ISBN Digital: 978-1-950466-24-5
Library of Congress Control Number: 2021902032

Conscious Capitalism Press is an imprint of Conscious Capitalism, Inc.
The Conscious Capitalism Press logo is a trademark of Conscious Capitalism, Inc.

Round Table Companies and the RTC logo are trademarks of
Writers of the Round Table, Inc.

EXECUTIVE EDITING	**Agata Antonow**
COVER DESIGN	**Christy Bui**
INTERIOR DESIGN	**Sunny DiMartino**
PROOFREADING	**Adam Lawrence, Carly Cohen**

This book is dedicated to my beautiful wife Dr. Veronica Ardi-Pastores, who has stood by me and supported me in every endeavor I had my heart set on. And to my daughter Zoey (code name: Z), who has been the inspiration to publish this book. The both of you are the light of my life and have made me stronger, better, and more fulfilled than I could have ever imagined. I love you both to the moon and back.

To my mother Revelina F. Pastores and my mother-in-law Lusia Ardi for being the prayer warriors for our family and for the selfless love and support that they give each and every day. Your undying support through the years has been the reason for my success and determination. I love you both very much.

To my hard-working dad Orlando A. Pastores, who I know will never read this book in its entirety but will buy it anyway to show his love and support. Don't worry, Dad, you have permission to use this book as a doily for your beer. Love you, Dad. Cheers!

To my siblings Rolan Pastores and Eileen Brown, I love you both more than you'll ever know. Best friends from cradle to grave.

To Tom Brady, Bill Belichick, and the 2001-2002 New England Patriots: just admit it—it was a damn fumble! Raider Nation for life!

To anyone who believes that you can do what you love for a living, make a positive impact, and be profitable at the same time. Keep fighting the good fight: we've got work to do!

CONTENTS

PROLOGUE 1

AUTHOR'S NOTE 5

| CHAPTER ONE | **AN UNUSUAL DAY** | 7 |

Session #2   7

Creating Relationships: Communication through
   Feedback in Capitalism   11

Conscious Consumers   12

But How Has This Changed Opinions and Relationships?   12

| CHAPTER TWO | **REFLECTIONS: OUR RELATIONSHIP WITH CAPITALISM** | 15 |

My Survey Work: Could It Help Me Understand Capitalism?   17

My Second Survey   19

Whole Foods: What Is Its Relationship with Capitalism?   20

eBay and Its Relationship with Capitalism   22

Google: Another Case Study   24

Starbucks and Its Story   25

Conscious Business and Capitalism   26

| CHAPTER THREE | **A HISTORY OF MY IMAGINARY PATIENT: HOW DID CAPITALISM START?** | 31 |

Session #3   31

Bad Capitalism? Good Capitalism?   35

| CHAPTER FOUR | **THE GOOD** | 37 |

Session #4   37

CHAPTER FIVE	**THE BAD**	45
	Session #5	45
	A Second Weakness: Change at Different Speeds	60

CHAPTER SIX	**CAPITALISM ON THE THERAPIST'S COUCH**	65
	Session #6	65
	Psychopathy and Capitalism	70
	Psychotherapy in the Boardroom	70
	The Government's Role in Capitalism	72

CHAPTER SEVEN	**THE RISE OF CONSCIOUSNESS**	75
	Session #7	75
	Changing the Story	83

CHAPTER EIGHT	**CONSCIOUS BUSINESS**	85
	Session #8	85
	New Business Models	88
	Principles of Conscious Capitalism	92
	Conscious Capitalism versus Corporate Social Responsibility	96
	Operational Values of Conscious Businesses	97

CHAPTER NINE	**CONCLUSION**	103
	Getting Capitalism off the Couch	105
	Your Tools	105
	Self-Report	106
	What Are Your Support Systems?	107
	Doing the Work on Your Own	107

| **BIBLIOGRAPHY** | 111 |
| **ABOUT THE AUTHOR** | 121 |

PROLOGUE

I am a marriage and family therapist. I share a building with many other medical professionals. The medical complex is situated in a very dense area of San Diego, California, and traffic can be terrible at times. It is ironic that my psychotherapy practice, a place that is meant to be a place of "zen," is sandwiched between the entrance and exit of one of the busiest highways in the city. Once you navigate the city traffic, you find yourself in the surrounding parking lots, circling and trying to find a free spot. From my office window, I can occasionally see and hear parking squabbles.

It's not the most calming introduction to a visit with a therapist. Just like litigants claim that they keep lawyers in business, conspiracy theorists would probably suggest that we purposely create a frustrating situation to exacerbate a person's mood, which could create an inflated sense of vulnerability and need for therapy. We don't do it on purpose, let me make that clear, but these introductory elements of agitation do help bring clients' authentic feelings to the surface early on in their visit.

I try to create a calming environment for people as they enter my office in an effort to counter the potential agitating trip to my door. There are smiling faces of emotionally intelligent staff that greet you when you open the door, comfortable chairs, calming music gently playing, abstract art in pastel colors, and calming scenes of secluded beaches and empty forests.

No matter how hard I try, though, sometimes the agitation doesn't waver when someone enters my office. You can learn a lot by the sound of a person's footsteps. When patients enter my office, I note their stride, breath, and any sense of heaviness in their demeanor. It all helps paint a picture of their genuine mood and disposition.

I remember a patient that came to see me earlier in the week. It was one of the strangest encounters I've ever had in my line of work. It was a walk-in appointment; he came in unannounced. I could hear his agitation in the hurried clomp of his feet in the hallway. By the time he arrived and I looked at his reddened face, I could tell he was anxious.

"Sorry I didn't have time to make an appointment. I just really needed to talk," he said sharply. "On top of the terrible traffic today, I stopped to get a cup of coffee at the place down the road, and it's like they are going out of their way to give people a bad experience. Story of my life, I guess . . ."

Before I could say anything, he took off his coat and made himself comfortable. He laid on the couch and propped a pillow up behind his head. He put his feet up on the edge of the couch and crossed them while simultaneously crossing his hands behind his head. It was as if he had done this several times before.

Despite his attempt to relax, he appeared to be a nervous wreck, restless and fidgeting. I tried to ask what his name was, but the patient abruptly cut me off and began to express a barrage of emotions that lasted for a good twenty minutes. The patient was hyperverbal. He talked nonstop and loudly.

"Listendocyouhavetohelpme. I need help. There's just so manyproblems." It was like turning on a faucet of emotions and not being able to shut it off. He clearly had a story to tell, and he began telling it immediately.

"I don't know who I am anymore," he exclaimed. "I, I'm misunderstood. I'm disconnected from everything around me and it's interfering in my daily—functioning. It's as if I'm watching a really bad movie about my life, and I just can't stop the train wreck that is about to happen. I've experienced a lot of trauma—throughout my existence—and it doesn't feel good."

I was intrigued by him and wanted to learn more. "Hmm, that must be a horrible feeling," I responded.

"Feeling? What are feelings? Lately I've been emotionally and physically numb. I have little reaction to things and have had trouble forming meaningful relationships. I really don't understand people anymore," he rambled. "People hate me, and they love me. I've been called everything from a savior to downright greedy!"

I was determined to find something he could identify as a moment of change or clarity. "I heard you say you don't understand people anymore," I said. "Has there ever been a time where you did understand them? Has there ever been a point in your life when you were happy? When you really felt like yourself?"

"When I wasn't confused about who I was, I used to be able to help people, make them feel better about themselves," he said. "I mean, I've literally changed people's lives. I felt like I gave people hope and made dreams come true. There was meaning in my life. But lately, I've been accused of taking advantage of people and not having a conscience. I'm riddled with grief and heavy guilt. Where did I go wrong? I feel like people think I'm a completely different person now."

As the patient continued, I began to use deductive reasoning to decipher a diagnosis. Could he be under the influence of substances? Had he suffered any seizures or brain trauma? Dementia? Anxiety? His dramatic mood swings met the criteria for a diagnosis of bipolar disorder or maybe schizophrenia.

The patient was describing a dissociative identity disorder or an identity crisis—what used to be called multiple personality disorder. He seemed to have an impaired awareness of his own actions, thoughts, physical sensations, and identity. He was detached and really didn't have a sense of who he really was. So what had happened?

My professional training kicked in. This might have developed due to his attempt to adapt to severe and prolonged trauma. Treatment would need to be an attempt to process the trauma safely and fuse the different identities that the patient was experiencing. He seemed to be yearning for a single complete identity where he felt more whole. He wanted a more consistent sense of self that highlighted his strengths and ability to make positive change in the world. How could I get him back to where he once was?

I knew I could help him, but I had another appointment coming in, so I said, "There is a lot of work we can do here. However, our time is almost up. When can I see you again?"

The patient seemed like he was in a hurry. He quickly popped back up on his feet and put his coat back on, without making eye contact with me.

"I will be back next week around the same time," he barked.

As he was hurrying away, I said, "Excuse me, I never got your name. What is it?"

Before he sped out the door, he answered, "I am Capitalism."

AUTHOR'S NOTE

When I set out to write this book, I wanted to create something anyone could pick up and read, but I also sought to create a commentary my audience could hopefully learn from. That goal led to the creation of a character—a therapist—loosely based on me and the creation of another character, my patient. While the pages you will read include fictional elements, they also include my years of professional experience and years of research. The examples I refer to are real, and all the words in the notes at the end of each chapter are nonfiction elements.

CHAPTER ONE

AN UNUSUAL DAY

Capitalism's ability to surprise me did not end with our first session.

"I guess you have found the world changing when it comes to how people see you," I told my new patient during our next session.

He looked at me. "That's a personal interest of yours, isn't it—how people see me and how that perception shapes their lives? In fact, it's what you studied."

My face must have showed my surprise because Capitalism kept talking. "You know where I like to go? College campuses. Young people usually see me as I really am—full of potential and possibility, just like them. There was a time when I loved sneaking into lecture halls when I felt blue. In the past, the business students—well, you should hear what they had to say about me. They were grateful, thrilled by the very fact I existed because of everything I could do."

Capitalism stopped talking and looked thoughtful. "Something's changed, though. Now when I visit, I sit there in the back of the hall and listen to challenges they face, and sometimes they say *I'm* the problem. Can you believe that? After all I've done. But *you* saw my potential when you were in graduate school, didn't you?"

"Pardon?" I asked.

"Well, we do know each other, don't we?" Capitalism asked, looking expectant.

I thought about his words for a minute. Since I'm a marriage and family therapist, many people assume that my "lane" does not intersect with business and economics. But that's just the thing, isn't it? Capitalism does not just have to do with money, economics, and business infrastructure. Capitalism is about people, psychology, relationships, and thinking. When I made this connection, I was getting my second graduate degree, and I became fascinated by the idea of capitalism and its role in society.

As I focused, Capitalism grinned. "You're remembering, aren't you? Beyond all the ways we've met—when you pursued college, created your practice, bought a house, there's the years you worked toward your doctoral degree in organization development—that's when we really connected."

"I guess that's true," I allowed. "But why don't I remember you?"

"Oh, most people don't," Capitalism said. "They don't think about all the ways I enter their lives. But you did think about it—more than most, anyway. One of your professors assigned your class a passion board project, to create a visual board of everything you had an interest in. She hoped that by seeing everything laid out like that, you'd see the connections between your areas of focus and get a better understanding about the research you wanted to complete."

I hadn't thought of that for years, but it was true; while researching for that passion board, I found out about Conscious Capitalism. It immediately sparked something in me. Here, finally, was an idea that married my fascination in people and the human condition with my interest in capitalism. Conscious Capitalism at its most basic is the idea that companies need to nurture and benefit all of their relationships, all of their stakeholders, and make a profit to stay in business.

Capitalism laughed. "Conscious Capitalism, right? That's when you discovered it and became so interested in it that you wrote your dissertation about it."

I allowed Capitalism to go on, and he seemed eager to do so. "You were captivated by the very idea: that there was a natural connection between the way we create our economy and the way we form relationships. You loved the idea that human relationships were about making the world a better place and that Conscious Capitalism recognized that I was a powerful force for making the world a better place."

I nodded. "I did find that fascinating, that capitalism wasn't just about numbers but about the world and about pursuing a higher purpose."

Capitalism stood up suddenly and glanced at his watch. "I have to be somewhere in a few minutes. Thank you for taking the time."

And just as quickly as he had arrived at my door, Capitalism was rushing out of my office.

When he left, I thought more about that moment I found Conscious Capitalism and thought more about my new patient. What he was saying was true: I know capitalism, and capitalism definitely knows me. Who doesn't know Capitalism? He is a part of everyone's lives. I immediately became aware of the strong emotions in response to my new patient and realized that I was experiencing something we in the psychotherapy world call countertransference. This can sometimes happen as a therapist transfers some of their feelings to their patient or if a therapist works with someone they know personally. When it does happen, it needs to be addressed immediately in order to most objectively help a patient. I jotted down a note to myself to address countertransference. As I made my note, the research I had out on my table caught my eye. The straight-forward research really spoke to me as I was reflecting on my reaction to my new patient and what he shared with me.

My research shows that traditional marketing tactics had been fairly straightforward and formulaic for decades. A company paid to advertise its products and services through "mainstream" media such as television, radio, magazines, newspapers, billboards, and/or resource-heavy in-store promotions. The "marketing mix" that a business deployed involved one-way communication (from the company to the consumer), delivering specific, controlled messages to targeted customers. A business decided what was important to a consumer and sold a product or service by claiming it met a specific need or want in a consumer's life.

Everything changed in the 1990s with the advent of the internet. The digital revolution not only introduced a new dynamic and complex marketing platform for businesses to incorporate into their marketing mix, but—and arguably more importantly—it opened up the world to instantaneous information about products and companies at the click of a mouse.

In addition to offering convenient access to company information (including financial reports and mission statements), the internet became a podium for anonymous, user-generated content and free discussion, which inadvertently changed the traditional marketing landscape forever. It wasn't long before consumer-generated review sites (Yelp, TripAdvisor, etc.) became the go-to resources for potential customers. As a consumer, even now, I almost never make a purchase without researching customer-generated reviews. The same goes for the restaurants, coffee shops, tire shops, and bookstores I choose.

Just as quickly as those review sites shattered the previous norm of prepurchase/previsit consumer decision-making, social networking sites burst onto the scene and became even more powerful tools for consumers. Facebook reviews are arguably a more popular go-to than Yelp these days.

The days where a consumer learned about a product solely through traditional marketing or customary word of mouth are long gone. Although getting a restaurant recommendation from a close friend or family member still holds quite a bit more weight than the opinions on social media, there's no doubt that online information from other consumers has replaced the carefully controlled marketing messages created directly by companies.

Where one person used to be able to tell a dozen or so people about their good or bad experience with a specific airline, that person now has an audience of thousands, if not millions, of people. Social media has amplified traditional word-of-mouth communication exponentially by providing a platform with the potential to reach many people all over the world.

People's "social circles" have become truly global connections, and customers tend to trust user-generated feedback. A Nielson survey in 2015 showed that 83 percent[1] of global, socially conscious consumers said they trust recommendations from people they know, and 66 percent of them said they trust the online opinions of other consumers.

Not all online feedback is positive, of course. Negative feedback spreads like wildfire on social media and can have a detrimental impact on a company. While in the past a dissatisfied customer may have told ten people, now they can reach thousands of people or more.

Creating Relationships: Communication through Feedback in Capitalism

As a result of these new digital platforms and the expanded reach of user-generated opinion, companies can no longer tightly control what is said and heard about them, and, as a result, brand personalities and reputations are vulnerable in a way they have never been. That means companies need to be proactive about remedying any negative feedback and must approach their relationship with the public in a new way.

Today, there is a genuine element of interactivity in the way businesses communicate with the consumer. They must "communicate" and not "market." Companies now need to listen to the consumer and respond to their needs, questions, and experiences or risk losing business as consumers shape the perception of the company online. This has shifted a lot of the power to the consumer and has expanded the number of platforms that companies need to monitor and respond to.

Consumers are now active participants in the communication process. In this increasingly conscious age, companies must not only have a higher

---

1   "Recommendations from Friends Remain Most Credible Form of Advertising Among Consumers; Branded Websites Are the Second-Highest-Rated Form," Nielsen, September 28, 2015, https://www.nielsen.com/eu/en/press-releases/2015/recommendations-from-friends-remain-most-credible-form-of-advertising/.

purpose and conscious mission to appeal to customers, but they must successfully engage in genuine dialogue with the customer to communicate that philosophy, and then live up to it.

Conscious Consumers

Running parallel to the technological advances that have expanded knowledge, shifted power to the consumer, and forced transparency and accountability in corporate America is a growing level of consciousness for society as a whole.

Studies show that a conscious consumer is more likely to choose to patronize a business that aligns with their own values. To attract these values-driven customers, a conscious business must effectively communicate a value alignment to consumers.

The shift from traditional marketing to inclusive and open communication with the public is no foreign concept to a conscious business because a conscious business is already philosophically poised to openly communicate effectively and deliberately with its stakeholders, including customers. Such a company is dedicated to authentically communicating and connecting with people around shared values. They naturally and honestly share what is true of their product or service.

You can find evidence of these characteristics by observing their public behavior (online or otherwise), reading their website and annual reports, looking at social media, and reading reviews. One of the more distinctive characteristics that a conscious business has is a rapid and appropriate response to an allegation or review that goes against what the company publicly stands for.

But How Has This Changed Opinions and Relationships?

While it was clear to me that attitudes of customers were changing and company strategies of communication were changing, there have been very few studies that gauge general public opinion of conscious business practices and philosophies. At the start of my dissertation project,

I wanted to know whether Conscious Capitalism was important to one group of stakeholders—customers.

In various studies, it is maintained that in a highly conscious society, consumers want to patronize a business that aligns with their values. I was curious if consumers were mindful of a company's consciousness and if a company's consciousness truly mattered to them. So I embarked on a study to gauge public opinion on some of the most widely recognized conscious businesses. I wanted to see whether consumers could identify certain businesses as conscious (whether they were familiar with the term Conscious Capitalism or not). I was also interested to see if those consumers placed value on the operational philosophies that conscious businesses wholly dedicate themselves to. For example, a conscious business is committed to creating a positive experience for its customers, not just a transaction. Do customers feel that? Do they recognize the effort? Do they even care? Can our relationship with capitalism and with a company be changed by what a business does?

And while it may be natural to assume that a conscious business would inherently communicate more effectively and transparently with the public, I wanted to see if that was in fact true. Were conscious companies communicating their values and foundational beliefs in a way that resonated with consumers and inspired them to align with that company based on a set of common values?

CHAPTER TWO

REFLECTIONS: OUR RELATIONSHIP WITH CAPITALISM

I went to my own therapist and advisor a couple days after my sessions with Capitalism, and we discussed the assumed countertransference issue and my background with the patient, and considered how to address the issue. My own conversation with a therapist mirrored in some ways my own work.

"My patient is a male, and I met him a long time ago," I told my colleague. "In fact, I didn't even remember him until he pointed out we had met before. And he brought out something in me. It's hard to explain. I want to make sure I'm able to help and stay aware of any countertransference so it doesn't affect my ability to work with him."

My colleague nodded and jotted something down in her notebook. I knew she understood. After all, it is something therapists need to have a self-awareness of. If a person in our care reminds us of someone in our lives or if we in any way transfer our emotions to the person in therapy, it can affect the patient-therapist relationship and can impact the quality of care received.

"If this is someone you know," my therapist asked, "is this someone you should work with? Would it be better for you to encourage this person to work with a different therapist?"

I hesitated, wondering how to explain Capitalism to her. "Well," I said slowly, "this person is extremely well known. It would be hard for him to find a therapist who was entirely unfamiliar. So he could run into this problem again with the next therapist. I do feel I can help; I just want to make sure I can really support him."

My therapist nodded. "That makes sense."

For the remainder of my session, we discussed my concerns and how to support my unnamed patient.

"Have you considered keeping a journal?" my therapist asked toward the end of our time together. "In addition to our own sessions, if you could capture in some private way your own reflections and concerns, that might help you stay self-aware. And if anything came up in your private writing, we could review it."

The minute she said that, I knew she was right. When I was looking over my dissertation and notes, I remembered how much I enjoy writing and how much clarity I always gained from it.

On the way home from my session with my therapist, I stopped by a bookstore and picked up a blank journal and some pens (yes, I am old school and like to *write*).

When I got home, I put my new supplies on the desk in my home study, ready for my first journal entry. While I was tidying up my space, I noticed that I had left my dissertation and notes out. I sat down and continued to read what I had written.

My Survey Work: Could It Help Me Understand Capitalism?

I set out to survey a random sample of people to see if businesses' consciousness really mattered to them. So I released an online survey first in 2013 and then again five years later, comparing the results. I collected 200–250 responses for each survey. Each time, the participants ended up being very close to a fifty-fifty split between male and female, were evenly dispersed across the country, represented the entire spectrum of household incomes, and mostly fell between eighteen and fifty-four years old. Overall, there was a wide representation of the consumer base.

By the time I designed the survey, John Mackey and Raj Sisodia (the founding fathers of the Conscious Capitalism movement) had identified many companies that were deemed "conscious." I started with this list of companies. Since I was most interested in how informed the consumer base was about these companies' philosophies, I focused on the companies that were most active on social media. I chose this approach because when a company is committed to communicating with their audience and doing it frequently (social media being the most used vehicle to accomplish this today), a consumer is more likely to be familiar with the company's brand personality and core philosophies.

The ten brands I chose to focus on were Amazon, Google, Starbucks, Whole Foods, eBay, Jet Blue, Southwest Airlines, BMW, Toyota, and IKEA—all companies that were deemed by the Conscious Capitalism movement to be "conscious." I asked questions in a few different ways. First, I gave respondents the opportunity for word association. I showed them a company's logo and asked for what words came to mind when they saw it. For example, I showed them the Starbucks logo and let them respond however they wanted—positive, negative, or neutral. Then I asked participants to rate each brand on an agreement scale for each operational value of Conscious Capitalism. We will talk about these operational values later in this book. For now, it is enough to know that by operational values, we're talking about the measurable, observable actions that result in a company being conscious.

Within the four tenets of conscious business practices (Higher Purpose, Stakeholder Orientation, Conscious Leadership, and a Conscious Culture) there are seven *operational* values that conscious businesses share:

1. Conscious businesses have low employee turnover.
2. Conscious businesses have very loyal customer bases.
3. Conscious businesses have high employee morale.
4. Conscious businesses make a difference in the world.
5. Conscious businesses give exceptional experiences to their customers, not just a transaction.
6. Conscious businesses are eco-friendly.
7. Conscious businesses value the interconnectedness between all stakeholder groups (value collaboration, connectedness, egalitarianism, cooperation).

To measure whether a consumer thought a company was conscious, I asked them to share their level of agreement with thirteen different statements that equated to these seven operational values. I asked people to tell me how eco-conscious they found a company; if they thought that a company likely has high employee morale and low turnover; whether they thought the company has a higher purpose and makes a difference in the world; whether they believed a company is likely to have a culture of collaboration and connectedness; whether the company has a loyal customer base; and if they felt that a company offered an experience versus just a transaction. Effectively, all of these questions were aimed at answering one thing: do you view this company as a conscious business? Lastly, I asked people to tell me how important these conscious values were to them as consumers.

As expected, most companies in the survey were perceived as conscious at varying levels. In 2013, Jet Blue not only came in last in terms of perceived conscious practices, but most people simply "didn't know" enough to answer one way or another (not a good sign for a conscious business, given their supposed commitment to communication and transparency).

My Second Survey

By 2018, fewer survey respondents were answering "I don't know" about Jet Blue and indeed about all companies. That leads me to believe that consumers are growing more informed with time, and after years of a company actively communicating its conscious philosophies, consumers had a more informed opinion.

Although I didn't intend to compare the consumer-perceived consciousness of each company, it was interesting to contrast the ratings from 2013 to 2018. In 2013, people rated Google as the most conscious of the brands included in the survey, followed by Amazon (see table 1). The airline brands came in last place both years.

Table 1. 2013 Results: Overall Perception That the Company Exhibits Conscious Business Operational Values			
Company	Highly Agree or Agree	Highly Disagree or Disagree	I Don't Know
Google	80.4%	8.4%	11.2%
Amazon	66.1%	18.4%	15.5%
BMW	65.0%	16.1%	18.9%
Toyota	64.3%	19.7%	16.0%
Starbucks	62.4%	24.4%	13.2%
Whole Foods	62.2%	12.5%	25.3%
IKEA	59.4%	17.8%	22.8%
eBay	56.9%	23.1%	20.0%
Southwest Airlines	47.5%	27.7%	24.8%
Jet Blue	33.4%	23.5%	43.1%

In 2018 (see table 2), Whole Foods sprung to the top of the list while Google and Amazon lost standing on the list. It was particularly interesting to hypothesize on the reasons why some conscious companies rose and fell within the ranks, according to my survey. For example, Whole Foods' rise in comparison to the others can easily be seen through the data as an almost straight shift from "I don't know" to either "agree" or "disagree." We can assume that the concept of a more informed consumer base is the reason for that shift.

Whole Foods: What Is Its Relationship with Capitalism?

Whole Foods has always been consistent in its messaging and prides itself on its conscious values. Its cofounder and CEO, after all, is John Mackey, who dedicates much of his time to teaching others how to build and maintain a conscious business. When my surveys asked individuals to describe how the brand made them feel, many people used words like "healthy," "organic," and "nutritious," which were the values that inspired Mackey to start Whole Foods in the first place.

Fig. 1. Whole Foods' Positive Word Associations

However, people also associated it with "expensive," "upper class," and "snobby." This is interesting because in 2015, a report in fact accused Whole Foods of having overpriced products. We are all aware that Whole Foods isn't necessarily known as an affordable market for many, but this particular accusation was about the market's in-store packaged foods (e.g., kale salad, meatballs, and other food from their in-store kitchen). Apparently, there were significant miscalculations in the containers' weight and, therefore, these items were priced higher than they should have been. Whole Foods' was accused of being an elitist, expensive market.

If you haven't read the story of how Whole Foods came to be, you should read their history on their website, or, better yet, read one of the books that John Mackey has written. It is quite a compelling and principled journey.

The company's purpose is straightforward: "to nourish people and the planet. We're a purpose-driven company that aims to set the standards of excellence for food retailers." Obviously, a claim that the company was mislabeling their products to the detriment of their customers did not align with their core philosophies.

In response to the accusations, the company took full responsibility for the mistakes and vowed to assess its operations to avoid any mislabeling in the future. Being a conscious business, they took it a few steps further. Recognizing that there is a perceived economic barrier for many people to shop at Whole Foods, the company hatched a new strategy to try to make their healthy, organic food more accessible to the public. They announced a new chain of the market called Whole Foods 365, aimed at providing fresh, organic, and healthy food at more affordable prices. The company listened to the feedback and tried an innovative course correction to meet the needs of the people.

Although the company took a temporary hit in the stock market after the initial allegations of their label manipulation, Whole Foods bounced back quickly and continue to provide great quality products to millions across the country.

In 2017, Whole Foods was bought by Amazon, and that shift had an effect on how people thought about the company. The news of the acquisition by Amazon found its way into the survey responses about Whole Foods, though not in a specifically positive or negative way. For example, some survey respondents just typed in "Amazon" in response to the Whole Foods logo.

Fig. 2. Whole Foods Neutral Word Associations. Notice that "Amazon" appears here after the companies merged.

Whole Foods doesn't actually spend a lot of its resources on traditional advertising and marketing, but it seems as though their consistency in messaging and the combination of two conscious businesses (Amazon is considered a conscious business too) may make for a promising future. Time will tell. If I do the survey again in the future, I'll surely be interested in those results.

Table 2. 2018 Results Compared to 2013: Overall Perception That the Company Exhibits Conscious Business Operational Values						
Company	Highly Agree or Agree	% Change from 2013	Highly Disagree or Disagree	% Change from 2013	I Don't Know	% Change from 2013
Whole Foods	67.69%	5.49%	19.97%	7.47%	12.34%	–12.96%
eBay	66.68%	9.78%	22.57%	–0.53%	10.75%	–9.25%
IKEA	64.10%	4.70%	22.81%	5.01%	13.49%	–9.31%
Amazon	61.05%	–5.05%	26.62%	8.22%	10.73%	–4.77%
Toyota	60.22%	–4.08%	23.86%	4.16%	15.92%	–0.08%
BMW	59.69%	–5.31%	22.62%	6.52%	17.42%	–1.48%
Google	55.19%	–25.21%	31.68%	23.28%	10.25%	–0.95%
Starbucks	55.19%	–7.21%	31.68%	7.28%	10.25%	–2.95%
Southwest Airlines	48.36%	0.86%	32.69%	4.99%	19.74%	–5.06%
Jet Blue	40.80%	7.40%	27.16%	3.66%	32.03%	–11.07%

eBay and Its Relationship with Capitalism

Along the same vein, in 2013 eBay, although still the second largest online marketplace, didn't seem to be communicating its conscious philosophies in a way that resonated with consumers. The survey reported that only about 57 percent of people considered it to be a conscious business, and 20 percent of people weren't familiar enough with the brand to give an opinion. By 2018, 67 percent of survey respondents described the company as a conscious business, and only 10 percent of people claimed they didn't know enough about eBay to have an opinion. The data could suggest that more people were informed in 2018 and that those people perceived the company to be conscious.

What happened? Well, in 2017 eBay went through a global rebranding. Not only did they double down on traditional advertising mediums (TV, radio, etc.), but they invested significant efforts into multiple social channels, focusing on Instagram, Snapchat, Pinterest, Facebook, and Twitter.

More important than their boosted effort to get their message in front of people is the fact that they clearly aligned their messaging with conscious business philosophies. Their new branding focuses on diversity, inclusion, self-expression, and global connectedness. On their website, they clearly state that they have a higher purpose: to accelerate an inclusive economy. From describing their "meaningful purpose" and commitment to being inclusive and values-driven to having a low employee turnover to plainly stating that they are making a difference in the world, the company is clearly trying to embrace the tenets of Conscious Capitalism. If eBay was on the couch in my office, I would assess them as having a very high-level interest in other stakeholders and likely to be a pretty healthy psychological system.

eBay is now even providing progress reports on how exactly they are making a difference. Their stated mission is to enable economic opportunity around the world. They also profess to work on behalf of their employees: "We employ extraordinary people who do meaningful work that has a tangible impact on the lives of individuals all over the world. And we aspire to make extraordinary things possible for each other, for our customers, and for you."[2]

Devin Wenig, the former president and CEO of eBay, is quoted as saying, "We are a company that lives its values. Our business is built on the belief that people are basically good and that commerce can be a force for positive change."[3]

I think it's safe to say that eBay is succeeding in communicating its conscious philosophies, and it is having a positive impact on consumers.

---

2   "2018 Tech Tour," Women Tech Council, http://www.womentechcouncil.com/programs /student-innovators/2018-tech-tour/.

3   eBay, Global Impact 2016 Summary, https://static.ebayinc.com/assets/Uploads/Documents /eBay-Global-Impact-2016Summary.pdf.

Google: Another Case Study

Just as with eBay, a lot can happen in five years that affects the consumer's perception of a brand—especially when we live in a twenty-four-hour media cycle and news races through the digital world so quickly. With that lens, I also looked at the companies that fell lower on the consciousness scale. The fall of Google on my list from the top to the lowest bracket, along with Starbucks, is also interesting.

In 2013, people associated Google with negative sentiments such as "big brother," "invasive," and "intrusive." However, in 2018, people were using much stronger language, including "evil," "spy," and "power."

Fig. 3. 2013 Google Negative Word Associations

Fig. 4. 2018 Google Negative Word Associations

So what happened between 2013 and 2018? In 2017, leaked memos and mounting complaints painted a culture and environment that was not aligned with conscious philosophies. Accusations of rampant sexism and antidiversity attitudes left Google in a reputation crisis. By 2018, the damage was done, and, according to my survey, it doesn't seem like they have quite recovered in the court of public opinion.

Starbucks and Its Story

Starbucks took a significant hit between the two surveys as well. Although there is a general opinion that Starbucks's products are pricey, people still reported feelings of happiness about their interactions and thought the product Starbucks provided was enjoyable. In 2013, 62 percent of people considered them to be a conscious business, and although some people used words including "expensive" and "overrated," there was a marked shift by 2018, when survey respondents were using words like "racist," "white," and "dubious" to describe the company.

Fig. 5. 2018 Starbucks Negative Word Associations

Just weeks before I sent out the survey in 2018, Starbucks was all over the news for a situation in which a Starbucks employee called the police on two African American men who were waiting for a third individual to arrive for a business meeting and were not purchasing coffee yet. Starbucks was quick to attempt a public relations fix and conducted company-wide diversity training, but the impact on consumer perception was swift and deep. Similar to the Google crisis, we'll have to see what the future holds in terms of healing the reputation wounds from that situation.

Conscious Business and Capitalism

Conscious businesses are not immune to poor reviews or negative publicity. One of the tests for true conscious businesses is how they respond in times of adversity. It is assumed that conscious businesses have a commitment to open and transparent communication with the general public as an important stakeholder.

I wanted to see if each company's efforts were working to communicate the foundational principles on which each company operates. However, the public perception of a company's conscious business practices is just one part of the equation.

To get a better understanding of how consciousness fits into the public's view of capitalism, I wanted to find out whether it mattered to them if a company had these philosophies. The results showed that those conscious business practices did, in fact, matter greatly to consumers when making purchase decisions (see table 3). Although I don't have proof that these survey respondents align their purchase behaviors with their values, there is research to support that assumption.

Table 3. 2013 vs. 2018: Importance of Conscious Operational Values						
	2013 Important	2018 Important	% Change	2013 Not Important	2018 Not Important	% Change
Eco-conscious	74.70%	77.99%	3.29%	25%	22.01%	–3.29%
Makes a difference in the world	81.10%	79.42%	–1.68%	19.00%	20.57%	1.57%
Really happy employees	83.70%	83.58%	–0.12%	16.30%	16.43%	0.13%
Positive "experience" versus just another transaction	91.90%	89.90%	–2.00%	8.10%	10.10%	2.00%
Very low employee turnover	60.50%	64.11%	3.61%	39.50%	35.89%	–3.61%
Loyal customers	89.10%	84.62%	–4.48%	10.90%	15.38%	4.48%
Values collaboration and connectedness between all stakeholders	81.60%	81.16%	–0.44%	18.40%	18.84%	0.44%

It is apparent from the surveys that a lot of what impacts a consumer's view of a conscious business is its public standing and how it respects its customers. A seeming misalignment between what a company does and what it claims as foundational principles is incredibly damaging, and may be more so for a company that publicly identifies as a conscious business.

Doing this survey raised more questions for me. Are our notions of companies just skin-deep, so to speak, and easily swayed by one news story? Can we really change how we fundamentally see capitalism?

It became clear to me that there's a tension in how we see capitalism.

On the one hand, we tend to see "big business" as "bad" or "greedy" or even "corrupt." On the other hand, we seem to want to work with businesses that are conscious and caring—so we do believe they exist.

Much of this tension seems to stem from the fact that we are living through a seismic shift in how we approach capitalism. Since capitalism affects so much of how we live and who we are, it's not surprising there's some discomfort.

To fully recognize the impacts of shifts in societal values, collective consciousness, and communication strategies between businesses and customers, we must understand and reframe the social contract that we have with capitalism.

The relationship between businesses and consumers has evolved throughout the years in response to changing societal values and an ever-increasingly knowledgeable consumer base. However, we are in a time where not all stakeholders within the systems have fully acknowledged the change and responded appropriately. For example, many schools of economics and business are still teaching an outmoded interpretation of capitalism, and some businesses still operate with a solely profit-driven mission.

Conscious Capitalism needs to be the standard for new business efforts as well as the foundation that existing businesses move to adopt. In order to do so, the whole system needs to acknowledge the shift and reframe the approach to capitalism.

As a therapist, I naturally lean toward a people-centered and relationship-centered approach. To ensure greater equality, clean air, and positive economic outcomes in the future, we need to get clear on what capitalism is and we need to make sure this relationship is working for all of us. Acknowledging that society and our relationship has changed is the first step to forging a healthier system.

By the time I had finished reading, I had almost forgotten that it was my night to make dinner! I quickly made a chicken stir-fry and ate it at the dinner table with my family, where we shared stories from our day. After I washed the dishes and kissed my daughter good night, I turned back to delving into my patient as well as my past. In fact, I spent a lot of time before my next session with Capitalism thinking about how to best help him.

To begin work with a new patient, I, like many therapists, do two things. First, I begin with the end in mind. That is, I work to establish goals with the patient, with the ultimate intention being to help a patient get to the point where they no longer need my help and have the resources and tools they need to move forward.

Second, when I speak to my patients, I also often ask for background information about what is going on in their lives. I take the pulse of their lives, from the people they spend time with to their jobs.

I see that Capitalism's world is changing rapidly, and of course nobody feels good if they think people think negatively about them. When someone thinks they aren't liked, the entire psyche breaks down. When a picture is painted of someone that is false, it is tough to shift that image—especially when that picture is shared with many. The end in mind for capitalism would be to change perceptions of capitalism. Capitalism could get off my couch, as it were, once people understood capitalism better and were able to relate to it in a more productive way.

I think a key part of that, in this case, is to ensure people see capitalism not just as an abstract "something" that is "out there" and affecting their lives but rather as a part of their lives that they have ownership in, which can help us all build a better world.

If our goal is to get capitalism off the couch and to forge a stronger relationship with it, my research shows how opinions of companies can be changed. Once companies start focusing on stakeholders and start communicating better with customers and audiences about what they are doing, a better relationship can be forged and some of the confusion and tension can fall away. Instead of confusion about whether capitalism is "good" or "bad," our conversation can move more toward a discussion of what capitalism can do as part of a larger society—what positive impacts it may have. For me, Conscious Capitalism is a large part of how we can create that healthier relationship.

But first, I needed to figure out how my patient got to me in the first place. I needed to learn more about his history.

CHAPTER THREE

A HISTORY OF MY IMAGINARY PATIENT: HOW DID CAPITALISM START?

Routinely when patients come in, one thing I will do early on in our sessions is to ask for background information about what is going on in their lives. This is not just small talk. How we think, or feel, or behave grows out of our past. In order to understand a new patient, a thorough biopsychosocial history must be taken. To understand that person in the present, we must struggle to understand them in terms of the past.

If a couple comes to me because they are arguing a great deal, and I explore patient history only to discover that one partner has been in an abusive relationship before or has suffered a specific type of trauma, that can impact how we proceed. I need to be aware of that fact as a therapist, and we may need to address and heal some of those traumas to help strengthen the current relationship.

In a session, I asked my patient Capitalism, "What is happening in your life, your world, and around you?"

"Things around me are changing pretty fast. I like to think I'm not changing much, though."

I nodded. Getting a patient history lets my patient and I put current challenges in context because we can draw a link between past experiences, the interpretation or internalization of those experiences, and current behaviors.

"Can you tell me a little more?" I asked.

Capitalism heaved a big sigh. "I hear all the time that we live in a capitalist system. Have you ever thought about what that means? It means Capitalism—me!—is the central system in society allowing us to achieve our goals. Whatever our personal goals are—whether it be sustaining a current standard of living, providing for a family, being a contributing member of a community, attaining financial stability—we can use the capitalist system to achieve them." He heaved another big sigh. "It's hard being a central system."

"No doubt," I reassured him. "You used the word 'system.' Let's explore that a little bit more."

"Well, a system is a set of *connected* things or parts forming a *complex* whole. It's not just me. We all exist through an infinite number of systems working (or not working) simultaneously. Our individual psyche is a system of complimenting and competing motivational drivers, reactions and responses, and levels of personal fulfillment."

"That's true." I nodded again.

Capitalism seemed to be warming up to his subject now. "Even each relationship we have with another individual is a system. The parts of that system include your shared experiences, expectations of fulfillment, and levels of enjoyment. For any system to be successful, or 'healthy,' there must be balance. For example, have you ever asked yourself 'What am I getting out of this relationship?' Or have you deemed someone in your life more of a 'taker' than a 'giver?' Balance is vital to the health of any system."

When he paused for breath, I chimed in. "Of course. Every family unit is a system, with people playing roles in an effort to achieve balance and happiness. Clearly, each workplace is a system of people and/or machines with specific purposes aimed at ultimate balance that produces a shared outcome. A fantasy football league, soccer team, or yoga class are each systems. From the macro systems like the planet's natural resources and its inhabitants to the micro systems like our household, our life is a constant endeavor for balance and the pursuit of symbiotic existence."

"Exactly," he agreed. "And no one system exists exclusive from another, however. Every day, there are an infinite number of systems operating concurrently, and they all impact one another. Have you ever been accused of bringing the workplace home with you? Or been told you bring your personal issues to the workplace?" His words made me think of my own questions about my own therapy session.

I chimed in: "The collection of systems in your life are not isolated from one another. Each system is impacting others. While some systems have more bearing than others, it's important to acknowledge the interconnectedness of our complex daily lives."

We chatted a little more about systems before Capitalism pointed out to me: "As a central system where everything is changing, how do I fit in? I don't live alone, you know. My roommates are a bunch of other systems, and we all need to work together, but as society changes, how can we do that? What are the rules now?"

He shook my hand before heading out. He was my last patient of the day, which is maybe why his words lingered.

When I got home, I looked around the systems in my own home: the food supply chain that delivered groceries for me and my family, the many systems that came together to let us watch my daughter's favorite TV show together.

After my family went to bed, I walked over to my work desk and opened up my journal. Inspired by everything that I have been reading about Capitalism, I started to write.

I have spent most of my professional life analyzing personal, relational, organizational, and family systems, trying to guide them into a state of balance, health, and success. The first and most important step is to recognize that we are all interrelated. Only then can we fully see a situation in its entirety. Although success can mean something different depending on which system you are focusing on at the time, the base formula for success remains a constant. A healthy, or successful, system is one that satisfies set or implied goals and contributes a certain value to the whole.

What does this have to do with capitalism? Quite simply, there is no other societal system more profound than capitalism. More than any other system that we have a role in, capitalism directly affects *all* other systems in our lives substantially.

Capitalism underpins nearly all other systems in our lives and allows them to function. This may seem counterintuitive to you, especially if you believe community or family to be the underpinning of your life, but consider this: capitalism impacts the field of study and career you chose.

The freedom that accompanies our capitalist society gives us a choice to follow our interests, skills, and ambitions into trades and specialties that are meaningful and that have the potential to earn us salaries that can sustain or improve our quality of life. That freedom of choice impacts the ability to provide for yourself and/or a family. Many people decide when and if to get married and have children based on simple economics, which is directly fueled by capitalism. Although "capitalism" may not inspire the same fuzzy feelings as those who are closest to us, we rely on it every day to support the relationships and very life we live.

Capitalism lets us satisfy our most basic needs, and some of our desires. It inspires ambition, growth, and creativity. It can push authors to publish books, artists to sculpt, engineers to design, and physicians to advance knowledge and healing techniques. It determines life spans and has helped us live longer and healthier lives. Moreover, our approach to capitalism and how we use it directly affects our personal and professional happiness and sense of fulfillment.

So let's take a closer look at capitalism as it exists today. The evolution of today's market landscape can be traced back to economist and moral philosopher Adam Smith. Considered a founder of modern economics,

Smith's 1776 magnum opus *The Wealth of Nations* is regarded as a fundamental work of classic economics and is still used as a teaching tool today. The book was, and arguably still is, extremely influential as it became the foundation from which economists and politicians have built our current systems.

At its core, capitalism allows for the voluntary exchange of goods and services between two parties, for mutual benefit—balance! Price is set based on quality and demand, and competition is encouraged. Competition and self-interest are terms we will be exploring throughout this book as we delve into the different adaptations of the root purpose and byproducts of this free enterprise economy. Adam Smith described self-interest and competition as the "invisible hand" that guides the economy. These are both considered the natural outcomes of a free market economy and also serve as forces of organic regulation within the system. The concept of "rational" self-interest is the term that explains the actions that buyers and sellers take during a transaction where both sides benefit, either intrinsically, financially, or both.

Smith presented capitalism as a neutral concept. Self-interest did not necessarily imply greed or immoral behavior, just a mode to reach your goals. A baker's goal may be to bake the best bread so that he can ask for a good price and therefore make the money needed to take care of his family. Wanting the highest price possible for a high-quality product is rooted in the baker's self-interest. His motivations are not rooted in greed; he wants to take care of his family. The baker may try different recipes or package the bread in a way that garners the most buyers, but all of his efforts are aimed at sustaining a quality life for his family. The goal of the woman who bought the bread may be to get the highest quality product for her hard-earned money and to not get taken advantage of by the seller. Her motivations are not rooted in greed either—simply a rational self-interest.

Bad Capitalism? Good Capitalism?

There is nothing either good or bad but thinking makes it so.

−*Hamlet*, Act 2, Scene 2

For a concept that, on the surface, seems so straightforward, the term "capitalism" can evoke wildly different reactions, depending on who you are talking to. Our attitude toward capitalism is rooted in the experiences we have, what we learn from others' experiences, and what our values and life goals are.

For some, capitalism is the root of all evil and the culprit behind many Americans' struggle and strife, the reason behind materialism and consumerism—something that will lead to the collapse of communities, economic stability, and spirituality. For one person, what is seen most prevalently of capitalism is corporate corruption and greed, so therefore they consider capitalism to be the instigator of those negative aspects.

On the other side of the coin, some people approach capitalism as an established method of opportunity and fundamental economic freedom. It conjures feelings of hope and promise. Job creation, creativity, and competition are essential ingredients and byproducts of a free market economy that can result in sustainable communities and fulfilled individuals.

Remember that at its core, authentic capitalism is a societal structure, and with it comes a social contract that allows for a voluntary exchange of goods and services for mutual benefit. Many social and economic problems today can be attributed to our inconsistent interpretations of capitalism. Not only does capitalism mean something different to different people, but it is a construct that has changed over time. It is a social system at its core, so we must regard it as a flexible and responsive construct that evolves with our collective values and societal needs.

No matter what emotions are brought to the forefront, when you think about capitalism, one thing is certain: it is the most significant system in our current society. In many ways it defines our individual psyches and micro and macro communities, and it influences our global standing as a nation.

Now let's go back to my patient. I believe my training as a therapist positions me to see dysfunction and trouble, whether it exists in a relationship or in a person's relationship with themselves. And I see signs of dysfunction in Capitalism. It has made me curious to look at this system, which affects so many, through my professional lens.

What can we see if we do apply some of the understanding I use in my practice to Capitalism? What if there is indeed dysfunction of some sort in the system?

CHAPTER FOUR

THE GOOD

We believe that business is good because it creates value, it is ethical because it is based on a voluntary exchange, it is noble because it can elevate our existence, and it is heroic because it lifts people out of poverty and creates prosperity.

—Conscious Capitalism Credo[4]

Session #4

"I have a question for you," I told Capitalism during our next session. "Last time, we talked about how you, Capitalism, are a system and part of the larger framework under which businesses operate and commerce lives. But isn't business fundamentally about people—people offering a product or service to others in exchange for another good or service of equal value?"

At that, my patient actually threw back his head and laughed. "Now you're getting it. Take a look at this."

With a flourish, he pulled his phone out of his pocket, opened an app, and slid the device toward me. On the screen was Capitalism, surrounded by people wearing work coveralls and some in business suits. Capitalism was in the center, beaming and with a huge cape around his shoulders, Superman-style. "You've found my superpower. It's people. I'm arguably the most powerful social system conceived because I leverage people."

---

4 "Conscious Capitalism Credo," Conscious Capitalism, Inc., last modified 2020, https://www.consciouscapitalism.org/credo.

Capitalism plucked back his phone and put it away. "And there is nothing more potent than the creativity, ingenuity, and innovation of people. Just look at our current technologically advanced environment to see evidence of the benefits of the ingenuity that was seeded through capitalism. What initiated the industrial revolution, which resulted in economic gains for the masses, gave birth to wide-spread investment markets, and fueled worldwide trade? What encouraged the manufacturing sector to bring to fruition innovations and ideas that resulted in increased production, communication, and transportation?"

Capitalism pointed to himself. "This guy. From factories to railroads, from vaccinations to public education, and from agriculture to automobiles, industrialization has moved us forward, and I was the conduit. Industrialization has led to an increased need for specialized education and training and, in turn, increased the access to education in order to feed the needs of the market. The jobs and training that came as a result led to the most rapid reduction of poverty in the country's history."

Capitalism grinned at me. "It sounds like you've been thinking about this out of our sessions, too. Have you been bringing your work home with you?"

I shook my head at my patient's sense of humor, but I couldn't help but smile. "Well, this is an intriguing topic. If I'm hearing you right, investment opportunities in manufacturing spurred inventors and entrepreneurs to create life-changing products and systems. The energy and economic activity that ensued lifted many people out of poverty, created jobs and educational tracts, activated a trade market, spurred additional innovation, and inspired a global economy.

"For generations of creative inventors and boundary-pushing scientists, you, Capitalism, have been the catalyst for revolutionary advances across many sectors. The creation of investment markets allowed the research and development of groundbreaking inventions like important vaccinations and medical treatments."

Capitalism winked. "Now you see my problem. I have this amazing power and have done good. People used to love me and understood my value. But something's changing, and now people call me the problem. What should I do? That's where I need your help."

We were both silent for a while.

We chatted some more about how a free enterprise economy allows people to assign value to that innovation and trade it freely. Having a system that elicits, expands, and harnesses that ingenuity is inherently good, and a well-run business can contribute to humanity in more impactful ways than any other organization in society. The entrepreneurial spirit, when applied holistically to a problem, can solve many of the world's dilemmas.

Capitalism was right, and a free market allows people to spend their money as they wish. It assigns an amount of power to the people and generates competition that can lead to innovation, prosperity, higher quality of goods and services, and an improved quality of life.

"I sure hope you can help me," Capitalism told me at the end of the session, as we were saying our goodbyes.

I had three more patients to see that afternoon, and when I got home, I took my family out to play soccer at our favorite park. After dinner, my wife and I began our daughter's bedtime routine, and before you know it, our spunky little two-year-old was fast asleep. I kissed them both goodnight and let my wife know that I would be up slightly longer.

I retreated to the living room and took out my journal. Once again inspired, I began to write.

Free market capitalism provides an open economy in which anyone is free to offer a good or service and in which goods and services are continuously improved through the competition between sellers of goods and services. Having multiple businesses provide goods and services also gives consumers greater freedom of choice and provides a system in which costs are regulated by supply and demand.

Imagine if there was only one brand of soda or only one company that made cars. The soda we drink and the car we drive would be controlled by only one business, meaning consumers would have less impact. Businesses would have more power to determine the costs and the quality of what they sell.

In contrast, capitalism gives the consumer power because we can choose which products or services we want to buy, which also puts pressure on businesses to comply with consumer trends.

Capitalism offers a dynamic system of interaction between consumers and businesses in which the development of products and services is creative and represents the interests of everyone involved. Therefore, capitalism motivates interaction between people and participation in something larger than themselves. Capitalism encourages evolution of the society in which we live because people are continuously inventing new products and services.

In the past decade, the evolution of digital and online technology has produced major developments in how people can communicate with each other, manage their lives, access information, and purchase goods and services. Without capitalism, these advances would not have been so forthcoming because the invention of new products and services is reinforced by a capitalistic economy that provides recognition and rewards for success.

The way in which capitalism is designed encourages entrepreneurship as well as both personal and social advancement. The opportunity for personal and professional growth that is created by living in a capitalist system must be underscored and appreciated.

There are many reasons why people are motivated to further their education, obtain job training, or increase their skill set, but the economic gain of such advancement is likely the driving stimulus. However, it isn't just about the money; our capitalist society also allows people to find their passion, identify their best strengths and talents, and gives them the freedom to think about what they really want to do—which in turn can enable them to achieve greater happiness, a sense of purpose, and true fulfillment.

Capitalism also encourages people to push through boundaries and do things they might not normally do. Since we are ultimately in control, the onus falls on us as individuals to take action and explore our own potential in order to progress. By doing this, capitalism also stimulates society to develop—to be creative, productive, energetic, and interactive.

Even in my own professional life, I have been affected by capitalism when it was time to create my practice. As a psychotherapist, I offer mental health services to patients who may be suffering from conditions such as anxiety, depression, trauma, anger—to name a few. A psychotherapist in private practice may very well choose the specific population he or she would like to work with.

For example, one of my colleagues, a clinical psychologist, worked with adults for more than ten years. She was an avid pet lover who owned two dogs and three cats. She was also part of different animal rights groups and spent her time volunteering for animal shelters. Given her current love for animals and her passion for helping others through psychotherapy, she decided to focus her private practice on assisting individuals and families who are grieving the loss of a pet.

Similarly, a psychotherapist who may be skilled at working with individuals with suicidal ideation may elect to do some research to find out which populations can benefit from his or her services. For example, in 2012, the Center for Disease Control came out with a report of the top professions with the highest suicide rates. Included at the top were farmers, fishermen, and forestry workers. There are inconsistent findings that mention dentists as more prone to suicide as well. As you can see, even psychotherapists can be creative in how they choose to specialize in specific conditions and populations.

I have been so inspired by capitalism and its potential that in 2013 I attended the Conscious Capitalism Conference in San Francisco. I was struck by Roy Spence's presentation, which included a quote from Aristotle: "Where your talents and the needs of the world intersect, there lies your vocation." Capitalism provides a social scenario in which we must continuously rise to meet the challenge of survival and changing social situations, which presents greater opportunity for personal discovery and evolution alongside the betterment of society.

Capitalism provides a light of hope, a beacon of opportunity for the industrious, an incentive to strive for what we want, the potential to actualize our desires and our dreams, the capability to choose and attain our goals, and the will to live to the best of our ability in ways that suit us. Freedom is not easy. But the alternative is having a bound system in which an outside authority deems the limits of our lives—and this is not in alignment with the capitalist and, dare I say, American spirit.

The freedom of the individual in capitalism is akin to the freedom of individual rights espoused by democracy, by our very American ideals. Historically, we tend to think that capitalism can only thrive in democratic societies or those that instill some degree of freedom of choice. However, the economy of China—a country that is politically communist—has experienced huge developments in capitalism.

China began to integrate aspects of capitalism in the 1970s, including foreign investment and privatization, and since that time its economy has expanded tremendously. In fact, according to the International Monetary Fund (IMF), in 2014 China surpassed the US in GDP and purchasing power, and now represents the world's largest economy. (To arrive at this conclusion, the IMF considered purchasing power parity, in which similar items in China cost much less than in the US.)

Regardless of the parity adjustments, China is a poignant example of how a country can develop and become more prosperous through adopting a capitalist economy—even when that country remains politically nondemocratic.

Further, the Chinese people approve of capitalism at very high levels—76 percent as opposed to the global average of 64 percent. Eighty-nine percent of the Chinese believe in their economy, and eighty-five percent feel that the capitalist economy will benefit the younger generations. In China, capitalism has profoundly boosted the economy and the optimism of the Chinese that they can do well and attain better standards of living. This is one of the many good impacts that capitalism has had on the world.

Capitalism has certainly had positive effects in other regions of the world as well, replacing existing outdated, authoritative, and overly hierarchical economic systems. Around the world, the expansion of capitalism has opened up global trade, stimulated economic growth, reduced unemployment, and provided pathways to higher standards of living and greater variety of choice—sometimes to populations of people who had never experienced anything but despotic government-controlled economies.

According to a recent report, economic developments fueled by capitalism have had a tremendously positive effect on a global level. In 1990, 37 percent of the global population lived on less than $1.90 per day. By 2012, that number had been reduced to 12.8 percent, and in 2015 it was under 10 percent. The source of this progress isn't a massive wealth redistribution program; it's massive *wealth creation*—that is, economic growth. Without the global-reaching system of capitalism, none of this progress would have been achieved.

So what is the good of capitalism? Among its benefits are a capacity for fair trade or equal exchange, profoundly expanded freedom of choice for consumers, a form of competition that encourages innovation of goods and services, an economy that is largely shaped by the demands and trends of consumers, and a system that motivates individual citizens to continuously advance their skill set, knowledge, education, and professional capacities. Capitalism is not a perfect system, but, then again, the idea of a perfect economic system is an illusion that does not exist on this planet.

CHAPTER FIVE

THE BAD

Capitalism is a double-edged sword, providing prosperity on one hand and turmoil on the other.

—Umair Haque

Session #5

The next time I met with Capitalism, I was running late. My daughter had a fever, and we had to make an appointment with the doctor. After dropping her and my wife off, I got stuck in traffic on the way to the office. Sitting among the other cars waiting for a break, I reflected on something Capitalism hadn't brought up: some of the negative press Capitalism had been alluding to.

It made me think of a patient I had seen. Years ago, a patient we'll call John came into my office with his husband. The couple had been having problems because John would lose his temper over trivial things, and his behavior was disruptive enough that it caused his spouse distress.

"We can't even go to the movies," John's husband explained in an early session. "He shouted at someone who checked their cell phone last week."

As we always do, we began our process by looking at patient history and by starting with termination in mind. What would it take for this couple to feel more comfortable moving forward? What tools and resources did they need to learn to get out of therapy? Together, we determined John was triggered by certain events, especially in cases where he did not feel in control. He was also determined to learn how to recognize those triggers and to find ways to control his outbursts before they happened.

My own graduate research suggests that bad things can happen to a company, and when they do, companies have a chance to turn things around. I saw this play out in my own research when I saw how customers reacted to Whole Foods with some negative reactions based on perceptions about price and value. By focusing more strictly on all stakeholders, including customers, Whole Foods was able to turn that perception around and create an even stronger business.

By the time I had arrived in the parking lot, parked, leaped out of the car, and sprinted to my office, Capitalism was standing outside my door.

"I'm so sorry to make you wait," I told him.

He waved my worries away. "No problem. I got the text from your assistant. I understand."

We both walked into my office and took a moment to settle down. Capitalism got comfy on the couch and looked out the window while I got out my pen and writing pad.

Finally, I cleared my throat. "Well, I think it would be useful to examine some of the problems and pain points we'll need to address."

Capitalism turned from the window and focused on my words.

"You mentioned you're a system," I began. "And every system has its weaknesses. Even our bodies have predefined genetic weaknesses, and many of us have weaknesses that can impact our emotional and mental health. And when one part of the system breaks down, others are affected."

"Have you seen that often?" My patient looked curious.

"Yes. Someone who is stressed may not only feel emotional distress but may start to experience physical symptoms such as muscle cramps or hypertension, but also emotional issues such as anxiety. Yet all the various complaints may be linked to the stress—the break in the system."

I was thinking Capitalism is no different than any other system and of course it has weaknesses. I wanted to test my theory. "Since you have stressed how Capitalism—you—enter deeply into every aspect of our lives, the impact must be extreme when something gets off balance. Can you address some of the vulnerabilities of capitalism?"

My patient was silent for a long time. "As I answer this, let's remember that capitalism is, at its root, about people—people offering a product or service to others in exchange for another good or service of equal value."

I nodded. I remembered my patient stressing that.

"Have you seen *American Greed*?"

I thought back to the enjoyable hours spent watching TV with my wife. "It's the documentary television series, right? The one about the history of America's largest financial crimes? I've seen a few episodes."

"Have you noticed a pattern yet? Many of the individuals highlighted earned educational, career, and financial success. Somewhere along the way, though, greed and a need for power take precedence, and egoism evolves. *American Greed* takes viewers along for the ride. Did you see the episode about Dr. Courtney?"

I shook my head.

"That was about the investigation of former Kansas City pharmacist Dr. Robert Courtney. Courtney graduated from the School of Pharmacy at University of Missouri, Kansas City, in 1975. A decade later, he became the owner of Research Medical Tower Pharmacy, in Kansas City and later still a deacon at an Assembly of God church in Kansas City. By 2001, Courtney became a successful pharmacist and entrepreneur. He owned several millions of dollars in stock and properties, lived in a large home, traveled often with his family, and donated hundreds of thousands of dollars to his church."

"Sounds like a success story," I said.

"Sure, at first. Courtney dispensed cancer medication in premixed bags to doctors. That saved doctors the trouble of mixing and measuring the drugs and allowed them to hook the bags directly up to patients' intravenous tubes. According to retired pharmacist Jim Frederich, 'A lot of pharmacists don't want to do that, they don't want the responsibility.'"[5]

"And this was in the TV show?"

"Yes. *American Greed* took viewers on the journey of Courtney's moral decline as he was eventually charged with diluting the cancer

---

5   Pam Belluck, "Prosecutors Say Greed Drove Pharmacist to Dilute Drugs," *New York Times*, August 18, 2001, https://www.nytimes.com/2001/08/18/us/prosecutors-say-greed-drove -pharmacist-to-dilute-drugs.html.

medicine he dispensed to cancer patients. Federal investigators say hundreds of cancer patients may have received treatment that was drastically weaker than what their doctors had intended. Courtney admitted to investigators that he cut the drugs' strength 'out of greed,' according to court papers."

I was silent, thinking about all the people hurt by these actions. Capitalism continued, explaining the trajectory of the story.

"Courtney's actions not only violated the trust between patient and doctor, but also damaged society—the system—as a whole. In December 2002, at his sentencing, US District Judge Ortie Smith stated, 'Your crimes are a shock to the conscience of a nation. You alone have changed the way a nation thinks . . . about pharmacists, the way the nation thinks about prescription medication, the way a nation thinks about those institutions we trusted blindly.'"[6]

Finally, Capitalism turned to me. "You work with people every day. Why do you think people like Courtney commit crimes? 'Greed' seems like a flimsy excuse for actions that hurt so many people."

"Well," I said slowly. "I've never spoken to Dr. Courtney, so I can't diagnose him. And I cannot diagnose everyone who has ever shown greed or destructive tendencies. But I can say, from my own professional experience, that when an individual or other social system is in dysfunction, it is commonly because there is a low level of social interest."

"Sounds like Alfred Adler. He was born in 1870, so a little before your time," Capitalism replied.

"I studied him in school!" I exclaimed. "The Austrian medical doctor, psychotherapist, and founder of the school of individual psychology. He made the concept of social interest prevalent in psychology. His approach and teachings have informed and influenced a large portion of psychotherapists today."

"Interesting ideas, too," Capitalism interjected.

"Alfred Adler's philosophy of social interest and individual psychology aims toward an individual reaching their maximum potential by

---

6 "Pharmacist Robert Courtney Admits He Diluted Drugs," *The Kansas City Star,* February 24, 2018, https://www.kansascity.com/news/special-reports/kc-true-crime/article705846.html.

striving toward significance. This often means an interest in helping humankind and contributing to their own communities. In fact, Adler would tell his depressed patients, 'You can be cured in fourteen days if you follow this prescription: Try to think every day how you can please someone.'" [7]

Capitalism looked at me and narrowed his eyes. "Really? You do nice things for others and you're cured? I'm a big believer in making a positive difference, but I always felt like that was a big claim from Adler. Do you use his ideas?"

"Of course. My psychotherapy practice here is Adler-influenced. I follow the logic that individuals were born with a drive to feel equal to other human beings—it's the root of Adlerian psychology. We inherently begin with passive feelings of inadequacy naturally because we are, by nature, born inferior to the rest of the world, meaning we are helpless infants that must be fed and nurtured into independent beings."

"Well, that kind of makes sense . . ."

I continued on. "We spend most of our lives unconsciously or consciously striving for a feeling of significance and belonging. In some cases, we obsess over our self-perceived inadequacies to the point where we develop an inferiority complex. This is a passive state of our psyche, but it oftentimes produces depression and anxiety, which can make people close down and shut off from society. On the other hand, people can overcompensate for that inferiority, swing to the opposite end of the spectrum, and develop a more aggressive superiority complex. In that case, people will feel a strong need for power, at which point greed and egoism are tantamount psychological drivers."

Capitalism seemed interested now. "Sure. That makes sense. I am fortunate enough to have lived for a long time and to have had the chance to learn and be influenced by some of the greatest thinkers. I was shaped by the early writers of capitalist theory—my parents, for all intents and purposes. I'd be a completely different system without them.

"At some point, I'd love to ask you more about your relationship with those early economist thinkers—your parents. For most of us, the early

---

7   Jon Carlson and Steven Slavik, *Techniques in Adlerian Psychology* (New York: Routledge, 1997).

phase of life heavily influences the inner goals and logic of our individual psyches. The family we are born into is the very first social group, or system, which is also part of larger groups in the outside world. Those very first years of our lives shape our psyche, so they are often the focus of psychological exploration. Were you born into a family unit? Were you born to a nurturing mother? Did you spend your early years in a stable, nurturing home? Did you spend your early time in the care of professionals at an orphanage?"

Capitalism looked deep in thought. "So you're saying we innately have a drive toward feelings of significance. Sometimes that journey away from the feeling of inferiority takes us too far, and we develop a superiority complex. When we are driven by a superiority complex, we feel a strong need for power. To attain that power, we will often invite greed and egoism to guide our decision-making, leading to self-centeredness with little awareness or regard for the world around us?"

"Yes." What I didn't tell him was that when I am treating someone in my practice, I look for elements of what makes up a person's level of social interest. It is a counterdrive in that it curbs the excessive need for power, which breeds greed and egoism.

Capitalism grinned, and I braced myself for what I was learning was his unique brand of humor. "You're saying social interest is greed's kryptonite!"

I thought about it. "That's a unique way of putting it, but you're right."

Capitalism stood up and looked out the window again. He looked almost shy, now that our session was ending. "Thanks for talking to me about greed without blaming me. Not everyone does."

With that, he walked rapidly out the door.

That day, I had an hour between patients, so after I completed my clinical note for Capitalism, I grabbed my briefcase, pulled out my journal, and began to write.

Individuals with high levels of social interest show cooperative, constructive, and contributing behaviors and often have a high level of sense of purpose and fulfillment. Finding meaning and purpose in life by participating in endeavors beyond oneself is a key aspect of social interest. I must admit that in my practice, I don't often have patients that I find have a high level of social interest. That's likely because those people who have a high level of social interest don't often struggle with anxiety, depression, or dysfunction—all elements that commonly drive people into my office.

In contrast, someone with a low level of social interest experiences systematic failures on multiple levels. From internal psychological functioning to relationships and work life, when an individual doesn't feel that they are contributing to a greater good, it bleeds into all other elements of life. Sometimes, it is difficult for individuals to recognize the problems that result in systematic dysfunction.

My role as a psychotherapist is to help individuals recognize their problems and find a way to correct them. There are four major steps I take with patients:

1. I establish a relationship with the patient based on equality and trust. It's important to make sure the therapist-patient relationship doesn't feed into any latent feelings of inferiority.
2. Through conversation and exploration, I find out what the patient's inner goals and drivers are.
3. Through more conversation, I help them to recognize what their inner goals and motivations are and help them understand how those motivations affect their decision-making and behaviors.
4. I ultimately guide patients to a point of awareness. When someone is mindful of what drives them to make certain decisions and how they impact others, they have the power to control how they respond to certain motivations. Helping them reframe how they perceive themselves and the roles they play in their life's systems is also key. They may not be able to see their impact on others, be it positive or negative. However, once they are conscious of these things, they are able to adjust, or redefine, their inner goals and approach to life.

The next appointment on my calendar that day was a woman I'll call Sue.

Sometimes low levels of social interest are not obvious in patients right away. When Sue first came into my office, it was because she felt unproductive. Sue was a successful senior executive and worked at her company for the past ten years. She reported excelling at work but not being satisfied with her personal life. She confidently walked into my office, well groomed, wearing a neatly pressed business suit.

I usually walk my patients to the door of my office and allow them to enter first. As the therapist, I usually sit on the single leather recliner. Patients usually assume I sit in this comfy recliner, so they choose to sit on the spacious sofa that contains a plethora of plush throw pillows. Without hesitation, Sue chose to sit in my recliner. This isn't necessarily an issue for me, but as a therapist, I was already in assessment mode. I was interested to learn more about Sue.

I smiled at her. "Good evening, what brings you in today? What's on your mind?"

When Sue spoke, it was with a serious tone and a look of concern. "I have been feeling unproductive lately."

"Tell me about it."

"Well," Sue began, with some embarrassment and anxiety. "I have about a dozen boxes that I haven't unpacked yet from a past move. It has been over a year."

I waited to see if she would say anything else. She did not. "I see. Why haven't you unpacked the boxes?"

There was a long pause. Sue looked down, not meeting my eyes. "Because I might unpack the boxes the wrong way."

I kept a straight face. "How so?"

Sue hesitated again. "If I unpack a box, I might come across an item and I won't know where to put it."

Sue's chief complaint intrigued me. In today's session, I wanted to understand Sue within her social context. I wanted to know how her perceptions were impacting her thoughts and behaviors.

When she came in, we chatted briefly about her job, and I began to seek out the context I needed. "What were your parents like? Were they also concerned about getting everything right?"

Sue considered. "They were very critical."

I made a note in my pad. "That might be difficult for a child."

"Yes." She looked down at her hands. "It was hard all the way through my teen years—until I moved away. They always told me I couldn't do anything right. After a while, I believed them, I guess."

"That sounds difficult," I said gently. "How did that make you feel?"

Sue paused for a long time, and I began to wonder if she would answer at all. "Unworthy. Unlovable. Unimportant."

As we talked further, it became clear that the criticism resulted in Sue developing low self-esteem, depression, anxiety, and anger. Sue's attempt to strive toward significance led to what Adler described as overcompensation.

"I just want to be a person who can contribute in a useful and valuable way," Sue admitted. "I want to belong and be capable and competent." Her voice remained calm and controlled, but I could hear the pain in her words. I could practically hear her primal screams inside her sentences.

Once Sue had confided in me, the floodgates opened. She told me about becoming a workaholic, working twelve-hour days with no breaks six days a week.

"I haven't taken a vacation in five years. I'm an aggressive leader and rule with an iron fist. I know what my coworkers say. That I talk down to them."

Sue's description of herself was overcompensation—what is visible to others when self-esteem issues, anger, anxiety, and other not-so-visible ailments are at play.

"Can you give me an example of when you might have been critical to a coworker—perhaps like your parents were critical of you?" I asked.

"Well, last week. A subordinate was late for work.

I asked why he was late, and he said he almost got into an accident. I replied, 'Next time drive more carefully!'"

"You mentioned this person was a subordinate?"

Sue sat up straight. "Well, he works on the team, but not on our senior leadership branch."

I found Sue's words illuminating. It was clear she enjoyed the power and attention. How could she not? She told me in some of our later sessions that she received promotions and substantial pay increases. Despite these accomplishments, she still felt unhappy. She withdrew from family and friends, stopped engaging in enjoyable/social activities such as attending church and volunteering at the local library. There were episodes of binge drinking that resulted in her first DUI and first arrest.

Sue's striving for significance (a desire to find a sense of belonging) went from feelings of inferiority to what Adler calls a superiority complex. In her efforts to strive for significance, Sue overcompensated. According to Adler, this is usually illustrated by someone's withdrawal from community/social interest/interest of others, and focus toward egoism, power, and greed.

Part of Sue's problem is that she found it hard to regard herself as an equal and adequate member of society. Her way was not producing the results she wanted.

Treatment for Sue would focus on having her understand that the causal factors were not as important as her idea and attitude that create her schema or worldview. In other words, her experiences in and of itself (i.e., her experiences with her critical parents) do not create pathology, but her interpretation of these experiences do. The process of healing required Sue to understand this process and strive toward significance through awareness and social interest.

Through the fostering of social interest, I would assist Sue in overcoming her feelings of inferiority, help her modify her view and goals (Adler would call this changing her lifestyle), and aid her in changing faulty motivation. This would lead her to feeling a sense of equality with others and becoming a contributing member of society.

Social interest is beneficial because it facilitates cooperation with people, provides a sense of belonging, and contributes to humankind. Empathy and compassion for others prevents selfishness, egoism, and greed. As social interest develops, feelings of inferiority and destructive behaviors decrease.

Eventually, Sue was able to gain self-acceptance. She reengaged in her church, even joining the church choir. She began volunteering again at the library and started practicing emotional intelligence at work. The focus on social interest, connectedness, and sense of belonging allowed Sue to feel valued, important, and competent. It provided a corrective experience, improving her self-esteem and decreasing her anxieties, anger, and depressive symptoms.

Although I wasn't assessing the health of the company she worked for or the impact she had on her coworkers, I can assume that her newly recognized level of social interest and her refreshed approach to cooperation and belonging led to a more harmonious and productive work environment.

Through my practice, I help to allow people to acknowledge their inner goals and reshape their approach to life and their role within it. It is essentially a reeducation process.

My third patient for the day, after Sue, was Brian. I felt Brian was almost at the end of his treatment with me as his symptoms had lessened, and I was pleased with his overall progress. When he had first come in, he was observably uncomfortable and sat fidgeting for a bit as we were getting acquainted. However, when I asked him what brought him to my office, he didn't hesitate.

"My marriage," he told me, not quite meeting my eyes. He looked out my office window. "I don't think it's working."

We talked about his marriage of three years. He couldn't put his finger on anything in particular but expressed how it was difficult to simply get through making dinner or running errands together without an argument. He kept saying it wasn't "working," which made me optimistic that maybe there was something I could help him fix to get his marriage back in working order.

Over the course of our sessions, though, it was apparent marriage was not the only thing on Brian's mind. When we started exploring all the other aspects of Brian's life, he showed a lot of frustration with his job.

"There was a promotion at work that I was sure I would get, but I was passed over," he told me in one of our sessions. "I don't get it. I have been working there for seven years and was told I was next in line. They just passed me over!"

His social life and friendships were another point of discussion, and one day he revealed that he played in a softball league. "What position do you play? When do you have games? Are you close with your team-mates?" I asked him. You'd be surprised at how much you can learn about people by asking them to describe their roles and activities in a team sport.

"I've been on the team for five years and play shortstop," he said. Then he frowned. "I haven't played that well lately, though, and spend a lot of time on the bench these days," he said.

"The guys on my team and I used to be pretty close," he said. "We would go get beers together after our games and stuff, but we don't really do that anymore. I guess everyone is too busy now."

Later on in that same session, Brian was talking about his marriage again. "The house doesn't help," he said, after describing an argument. "It's too small, and we don't have our own space. Maybe if we had a bigger house . . ."

It was clear that it wasn't simply his marriage that wasn't working for Brian—nearly every system in his life felt a bit out of order.

Regardless of whether it is true or not, when an individual doesn't *feel* that they are contributing to a greater good, it results in a low level of social interest. Individuals like my patient Brian have a deficit in social interest that diminishes their ability to experience a sense of belonging and connectedness with others.

After a few sessions with Brian, I helped him to realize that he was unhappy with his life because he didn't feel that he was contributing to something beyond himself. His low level of social interest had a negative impact on all the other systems in his life, from his marriage to his softball team, which, in turn, produced more negativity and failures—a vicious cycle.

In reality, it's not that he *wasn't* contributing to a greater good; he just didn't recognize his contributions. Identifying your value toward something beyond yourself is the first step in growing your social interest. Even acknowledging how your systems impact and interact with other people's systems can make a difference in your psyche.

With a little adjustment to his approach to life and mindset, he was able to feel his worth and value, which motivated him to do even more, to increase his level of social interest. Through a combination of a couple different active therapy techniques, we were able to identify where he felt inferior.

Only after he had that awareness were we able to reframe his way of thinking and see the positive and contributory impact he had on the many others in his life. He was able to associate his life experiences with corrected feelings of belonging and adequacy.

Once he began to recognize that he was, in fact, contributing to the common good and making a difference in many people's lives, his level of social interest grew. As a result, he gained confidence, moved away from isolation and toward prosocial experiences. His sense of belonging was restored.

It wasn't long before the systems in his life, including his marriage, were back on track and healthy. During this latest session, he bounced into my office and sat down, smiling.

"How are things going?" I asked after we had exchanged pleasantries.

"It's as if I feel like I am awake again," he said.

"And how are things in your marriage?"

His grin widened. "I couldn't put my finger on it before. I just didn't feel like I had anything to give to the relationship. Now I recognize how important I am to her and how much it means to her for me to really 'be there.'"

We discussed some of the changes he had been making in his life and how he was reaching out to people more. When we shook hands to say goodbye, I made a mental note about our next session. I wanted to discuss some tools he could use in the future; he was almost ready to stop therapy and continue on his own.

I had no more sessions after Brian and I drove home, picking up dessert. My family was hosting a dinner party to celebrate a young member of my extended family who had recently graduated from a business school at a New York university.

Dinner was wonderful, and I even got a chance to speak to the guest of honor. "Congratulations," I told her. Then I asked her what she was no doubt asked dozens of times that night:

"Now that you have this business degree and have learned so much, what are you going to do with it?"

I was wholly expecting an answer that would give me an idea of what industry she would like to be in, what her passions were, what fueled her entrepreneurial spirit. I knew she loved horses and animals of all kinds, so I was thinking she might open a veterinary clinic or perhaps some other business related to animals. Which made what she said so surprising.

"I'm going to make money," she quickly answered with conviction. "And lots of it."

"Okay," I said. "How are you going to do that? Do you have a particular idea in mind, or an industry you'd like to make a difference in?"

Her next words made me immediately realize my approach and understanding of the immense potential and freedom that capitalism provides us was not the most salient piece of education my dear cousin had received at her college.

"Oh, I don't really care what I do or how I do it," she continued breezily. "It doesn't matter to me if I work in the most boring industry there is. I just know I want to be rich."

Ouch! She said it plainly and with such fervor that I could only smile and say, "Well, good luck with whatever you find yourself doing."

She may very well come out of that belief system (I hope!) after the power of her business school's teachings wears off, and the excitement of graduation wanes. I fully understand how empowered and, at times, entitled fresh college graduates can feel. However, it was glaringly clear to me how downright misguided she had become in terms of what role she could and would play in our economy.

Her university professors and the curriculum they focused on certainly didn't offer her the tools she needed to feel impassioned by contributing to the common good, or to feel excited for the innovation potential of the free market. She was taught that the most important thing, if not the *only* important thing, about business is profit.

Her words stayed with me long after all the guests had left and after I had helped my wife tidy up our dining room. As my wife graded papers and prepared for her next lecture, and my daughter slept, I turned to my journal to work out what the day had brought me.

An individual with a low level of social interest can be the weak link in multiple simultaneously interworking systems in life. Brian's deficiency was negatively contributing to each of his systems: marriage, household, office dynamics, softball team, etc.

How are Brian and Sue linked to capitalism? While we can't diagnose capitalism or ask the system to hop on a therapist's couch for counseling, we can examine the individuals within the system. When they are dysfunctional, the whole system is dysfunctional, just like Brian's troubles affected his marriage (a system) and Sue's challenges affected her work relationships. Capitalism is a system comprised of people who are all vulnerable to weaknesses within their own psyches and potentially misguided goals and motivations.

It can become a self-fulfilling prophecy, too. Although capitalism was intended as a neutral concept to spur economic growth, innovation, and freedom, some people consider capitalism to be a profit-driven system, steeped in philosophies of individualism, saturated with greed and egoism, fueled by private property, and exacerbated by an unregulated economy. When individuals see capitalism this way, they can let greed become their sole motivation instead of being driven by purpose. Greed, intertwined with egoism and self-centeredness, is what they think capitalism just "is," and these individuals become weak links in the overall system. In turn, their weakness weakens the whole system.

When Brian didn't see himself as contributing to something bigger than himself, his perceptions resulted in dysfunction across the board. Similarly, when a company's leaders don't enrich their missions with benefits to the greater good, or contributions that better society in some way, it can result in economic turmoil and financial disaster.

Don't get me wrong: financial profit is absolutely necessary for the healthy function of a free market economy. However, a solely profit-based motivation breeds greed and egoism and leads to unhealthy, systematic dysfunction. Milton Friedman, one of the most influential economists of the twentieth century, reinforced the notion that profit should be the sole motivation of business. He didn't ignore the benefit of the greater good, however. He believed that a profitable business will ultimately be beneficial for society.

Even today, foundational economic teaching relies heavily on the often-times misinterpreted approaches to profit motivation put forth by early economists. As reported in an article in *Business Ethics Quarterly*, some business ethics textbooks still interpret the Smith and Friedman doctrines of self-interest and the pursuit of profit in the following way: "people should pursue their self-interests; businesses should do whatever improves their financial position, even if others are harmed; and in some way the 'invisible hand' ultimately makes the effects of such actions right for society."[8] Some have suggested that business school education may contribute to unintended consequences of students' attitudes toward greed.

Academia in the areas of economics and finance have consistently preached the conventional themes of maximizing shareholder value and competing against other stakeholders. This may have caused new generations to believe that business's sole purpose is to do whatever it takes to meet financial bottom lines, even to the detriment of others, and maybe even that businesses were free from any sense of morality. My cousin seems to be on this trajectory.

A Second Weakness: Change at Different Speeds

When morality comes up against profit,
it is seldom that profit loses.

−Shirley Chisholm

Since capitalism was established as our economic system, we have endured significant societal changes that have substantially altered not only our commercial operation but our viewpoints on commerce as a whole. We are now mindful of the untallied cost of capitalism in the form of the depletion of natural resources, workforce exploitation, sustained and growing wage gaps, corporate fraud, and diminution of public trust in companies and their leadership. In the "Digital Age" (also referred to the "Information

---

8   Harvey S. James and Farhad Rassekh, "Smith, Friedman, and Self-Interest in Ethical Society," *Business Ethics Quarterly* 10, no. 3 (2000), https://doi.org/10.2307/3857897.

Age"), we get our information differently than we used to. We demand transparency and responsibility from the corporate world.

Some people have blamed capitalism for recent societal challenges resulting in recessions, economic turmoil, oppression, substantial moral delinquencies, and a society hyperfocused on materialism and personal financial gains. I don't disagree that the system has been in massive dysfunction at times, but I don't think the system is to blame. When you have a plumbing leak in your house, you don't blame the entire concept of indoor plumbing, do you? When you get a flat tire, you don't claim that the entire concept of an automobile is flawed, right?

What is to blame is the interpretation, approach, and utilization of a system that is vulnerable to weakness. For instance, if your interpretation of the sole purpose of a free market economy is for some people to get rich, as evidenced in the dated and incomplete teachings still in play at some prominent business schools, therein lies the weakness in the system.

Each event we experience in life produces automatic thoughts, which lead to feelings, which lead to behaviors and subsequent consequences. If we are able to change our involuntary thoughts and reframe the feelings that follow, we are then able to change everything that comes next.

As I wrote those words, I couldn't have realized how prescient they would prove to be. A few weeks after that journal entry, I found myself in my doctor's office, being asked to take some medical tests "as a precaution."

"They're just a precaution," I reassured my wife, but a few days later I got a call from a concerned-sounding doctor.

I was diagnosed with a heart problem. "Surgery is your best option," I was told.

The months-long recovery process was rough since I have a wife and baby that rely on me. I couldn't run after my daughter, couldn't help as much around the home. We were all worried: would I get better? Would the treatment work? Instead of seeing patients, I attended cardiac rehabilitation sessions and doctor's appointments. The one spot of hope was that my patients were very kind and understanding when I needed to reschedule. Capitalism sent a card with a picture of a patient covered head to toe in bandages. Inside, he had written, "Get better, Doc. Your favorite patient will still be around once you're better. And remember what system has allowed hospitals to be built and medical practices to function." My wife put the card along with the others I received in the living room, where I would see them every day.

The slow recovery and ongoing rehabilitation were a test of my patience, to say the least. I often wondered if my heart would ever recover. How long would I live? Would my wife be okay? Would I get to see my daughter grow up? In the midst of anticipatory anxiety, frustration, sadness, and ugly crying, I asked myself, "Is this really my life?"

I had to change how I thought about my health and start to shift how I lived my life with the new reality of my illness.

Then, one night, I glanced over at my wife, who was asleep beside me. At that moment, my eyes were opened and my heart was filled with gratitude and hope. The feeling came out of nowhere, a mindset shift, after many months of struggle. I was not expecting and cannot exactly explain where this realization came from or what sparked it in that specific moment. But I do know it changed how I viewed my situation.

I can overcome any hardship with this woman by my side, I thought in that moment. Our courtship and marriage for the past thirteen years has been through college, distance, heartbreak, financial instability, health scares, and now the struggles and blessings of parenthood. I do know this: God has never let me down and neither has my wife. So I chose to reframe my perspective and instead I felt the need to write this note to my wife:

Dear Vero (Veronica),

I am thankful for everything you do and all that you have sacrificed. I wouldn't trade lives with anyone else because what I have right now with you is so good. Today, on our 7th wedding anniversary, I ask myself again with so much joy, "Is this really my life?"

When we change our point of view, the facts remain the same, but we can choose to intentionally shift the way we look at those same facts. Reframing is used in many disciplines to create shared understanding, meaning, and motivation. Reframing is a common practice in psychotherapy, where it is used to help individuals reenvision their role in their respective world. Reframing in this context allows people to focus on a perspective rich in social interest and results in positive change. For me, reframing allowed me to climb out of fearful thoughts and worry to a new appreciation of what I already had before me. My wife had always been right there beside me every night. But when I reframed and looked at her with new eyes, it impacted my entire relationship with my condition and with her.

In our wider society, there is ample evidence of reframing and massive change, but it's possible that the way we collectively use the capitalist system hasn't evolved at the same pace as society. So much has changed in our lives over the past few decades. Our industrial focuses have shifted. What we manufacture has changed. The way we bank, invest, and transact business is completely different than even ten years ago. Our collective mind has shifted, and we are redefining the "American Dream." Most importantly, we have become a society that is mindful and conscious of our impact on others—from our communities and around the globe. We are more enlightened on issues of waste, environmental impact, labor, and human rights. It is time for us to use our economic system accordingly.

Capitalism as it is currently perceived and taught by most, with its profit-driven motives and egoist nature, does not match the collective psyche of society. When greed and profit are considered to be the foundation of how our economy operates, it is doomed to dysfunction and sickness.

Just as the psychotherapy methods described in this chapter aim to reframe and reeducate people on how they view their roles in life and increase their levels of social interest, we can reframe and reeducate people on the way we approach capitalism and redefine what our roles are within the greater economic/social system.

CHAPTER SIX

CAPITALISM ON THE THERAPIST'S COUCH

In a positive paradigm, the healthiest state isn't just one that minimizes pathologies, but one that maximizes potential.

–Umair Haque[9]

Session #6

As I got better, I was able to return to my practice. I knew my next session with Capitalism would be challenging because we'd have to tackle dysfunction.

My patient walked in, looking relieved to see me well. After asking me politely about my health, he referred to our last session. "I guess we're going to discuss more of that, aren't we? What happens when Capitalism is unhealthy?"

I nodded. "It's important. Capitalism is a system that, when healthy, can provide immense growth and prosperity, but, when the system is unhealthy, it can be unstable and can cause economic collapse. A sole focus on profit and the resulting byproduct, greed, creates the ideal environment for corporate manipulation and unethical business practices."

"It gets ugly," Capitalism agreed.

"Yes. But it's not really you, is it? Capitalism gets ugly when individuals who are part of the system are not psychologically healthy. Dysfunction settles in rapidly and the system breaks down, to the detriment of the whole."

---

9   Umair Haque, *Betterness: Economics for Humans* (Boston: Harvard Business Review Press, 2011).

"People forget that," my patient piped up. "But each system is made up of individuals, and when the individual's psychological health is in trouble, a domino effect ensues. I don't know if you remember when executives from once iconic institutions like Enron, WorldCom, and Tyco were caught and convicted of engaging in illegal business practices. It all happened around the same time, too."

"What was that like for you?"

Capitalism looked genuinely upset. "It was terrible. Executives at Enron fooled regulators for *years*. Fake holdings, unethical financial reporting practices, off-the-books accounting—all in an effort to boost their perceived value in investors' eyes. After the destructive practices crumbled the company in 2001, several of Enron's executives were slapped with a variety of charges, including conspiracy, insider trading, and securities fraud. The collapse affected thousands of employees and disrupted the stock market."

"And it happened with WorldCom again, didn't it?"

My patient nodded. "WorldCom was once the second largest long-distance telephone service provider in the country, but by the early 2000s executives were hiding decreases in company revenue to maintain the value of the company's stock and keep investors happy. The CEO, Bernard Ebbers, was convicted of orchestrating an $11 billion fraudulent accounting scheme and was sentenced to twenty-five years in prison."

"And Tyco was around the same time?"

Capitalism nodded again. "They were a huge electronics giant and one of the largest corporations in America. They seemed too big to fail. You can imagine the shockwaves sent through the international financial markets when they collapsed in the early 2000s. The company's executives were manipulating financial documents and filing fraudulent claims about the company's financial performance. Again, all to keep investors happy. Corporate greed and excess, again. Tyco executives were charged with grand larceny for taking hundreds of millions of dollars from the company."

"And you felt blamed for it?" I asked, watching Capitalism.

"Have you read the report by the Institute for Policy Studies? The one that found that about 40 percent of the highest paid CEOs in the United States between 1992 and 2013 were fired for fraudulent behavior? Between reports like that and news headlines about corporate greed, it's easy to blame capitalism and to label jailed executives as somehow inherently 'bad' or 'evil.' Do you think that's true?"

Capitalism looked distressed, and I reassured him. "I think that approach is inaccurate. Business leaders are not generally bad, but they do suffer some of the same challenges many of my patients do."

"Like what?"

"For all of us, our perception of our role, value, or impact in our systems impacts our social interest. A patient of mine may feel unhappy in a marriage, for example, because they feel unappreciated. The negative perception of their role, impact, or lack of value within their system in turn makes them have low social interest. Feelings of unappreciation can lead to isolation from others, and one can ultimately turn their back on society."

My patient looked almost hopeful. "Do you think that applies to me, too?"

I nodded. "Yes. In much the same way, our perception of capitalism and our own role or value in it affects our social interest and thus how we approach our roles, personal responsibilities, and purpose as part of the free market system. When business leaders responsible for key decisions see their value or role as only one of profit, for example, they may see their purpose within the free market to pursue profit at any cost."

When Capitalism left my office that day, he walked with a lighter step. I finished up a shortened day and came home, feeling more tired than usual. I was touched and delighted when my wife and daughter greeted me at the door. My wife had prepared a special supper and led me to the living room for a "surprise."

I gasped when I saw what she had worked all day long to create. She had set aside a small part of our living room to be an office, so I could work quietly near her as she read and relaxed in the evenings. She had even put a vase of fresh flowers by my desk.

"It would be nice for you to be closer and for me to keep an eye on you as you write." She kissed my forehead and shooed me to my new spot to write.

I sat down and smiled, grateful for her gesture and eager to write.

When economics and capitalism is taught with an emphasis on profit, it can create a culture engulfed by fierce competition, fueled by pressures to meet the bottom line and keep investors happy.

The 2008 financial crisis, the worst economic disaster since the Great Depression, was a direct result of a capitalist system that was poisoned by greed and profit-driven motivations. The crisis played a significant role in the failure of key businesses, declines in consumer wealth estimated in the trillions, a downturn in economic activity that led to the Great Recession of 2008–2012, and a global financial fallout. The regulations that the US government enforced (and didn't enforce), financial industry loopholes, shady shell games, risky home buyers, and loose lending regulations all played a part in the global crisis. The silver bullet culprit for the crisis is widely debated, and it is likely a combination of all of the above creating a perfect storm. One thing is for certain, though: every step taken by each and every entity involved was steeped in greed and nearly devoid of social interest.

We are all an either active or inactive part of the economic system in some way. And that means we all have the potential to contribute to it in positive or negative ways. The exciting thing is that we can use our role to change the whole.

So where did we go wrong in the economic collapse of 2008–2009? The Financial Crisis Inquiry commission released a report in 2011 on the cause of the crisis. They reported that the crisis was avoidable and caused by financial firms acting recklessly, households giving in to materialism and purchasing homes that they couldn't afford, Wall Street playing games with financial markets, policy makers' detrimental lack of understanding of the complex financial systems, and ethics violations at every level. Although it was arguably not a failure of the free market system, it could be argued that it was a result of amplified greed running rampant in the banking and finance industries, which is a direct result of profit-driven capitalism.

In authentic capitalism, goods and services are exchanged freely, and the value for goods and services offered is determined by a market interaction. If players in our capitalist system artificially created the value of a product (be it a stock price, house, or a bundled mortgage loan) at the expense of another human being, or entity, that is a manipulation of the system and should not be considered a representation of authentic capitalism. Remember Smith's promotion of rational self-interest? There was nothing rational about the self-interest of the players responsible for the financial crisis. It was irrational, egotistical profit-driven individuals and organizations.

Remember how we described capitalism with the example of the baker selling his product for a good price and the buyer wanting to get good-quality product for his hard-earned money? The baker is a part of the system known as capitalism, and the system affects him just as much as he impacts the system. For example, if the baker's purpose became profit alone, he could raise his prices. He could use filler ingredients that may be cheaper for him to buy but that are developed in ways that hurt the environment. He could hide the fact that he is using those filler ingredients from the customer and, in effect, misrepresent the quality of his product.

What he may not realize in the short term is that by exploiting the system (artificially raising the prices, acting without the interest of common good), he ultimately harms himself. How? If he cheats someone or cheats the system, he makes himself vulnerable. For example, if his profit-driven tactics were exposed, the trust between the baker and the customer would be broken. Once customers find out that the exchange is no longer mutually beneficial, he can lose customers. His reputation would be tarnished, and the livelihood that he had initially depended on to take care of his family would be threatened. There is some truth to the age-old adage "what goes around comes around." The behaviors of individuals within the system of capitalism ultimately come back around to that individual. When someone isn't acting for the benefit of the greater good, they suffer just as much as others in the long run.

Although a capitalist system doesn't by nature lead to greed, marginalization, and exploitation, those that have the potential to create a flourishing free market also have the power to introduce a weakness to the system that spreads throughout like a plague. Clive Boddy, an expert in leadership and organizational behavior, places keen blame for the financial crisis on corporate leadership. He stated that corporate financial scandals have assumed epidemic proportions, and companies with previously unblemished, and even dignified, reputations have been brought down by the misdeeds of a few of their leaders. The onset of the global financial crisis has thus led management researchers to be increasingly interested in the various aspects of dark leadership in an attempt to explain the current financial and organizational turmoil around the world.

Psychopathy and Capitalism

One truly ugly byproduct of profit-driven capitalism is the "corporate psychopath." The concept of the corporate psychopath marries the terms "psychopath" from the psychological literature with the term "corporate" from the area of business to denote a psychopath who works and operates in the organizational setting. Boddy suggested that these "corporate psychopaths" may have been responsible for the global financial crisis. These individuals exhibit the same characteristics as psychopaths identified in clinical psychology in that they lack a conscience, have few emotions, and display an inability to have any feelings, sympathy, or empathy for other people. They manipulate others to further their own agendas. Given the definition, a person who is a psychopath certainly lacks a healthy level of social interest considering that social interest encompasses elements of empathy, compassion, and cooperation. Again, weak psychological health of any system is a root cause of dysfunction.

Psychotherapy in the Boardroom

I have always believed that organizations should have a resident psychotherapist. Treating the psychological health of a company is possible, just as we do with individuals, since the psychological health of a company is the sum of the health of its people. An organizational psychotherapist can improve the mental health of an organization and move organizational members toward a state of cognitive harmony. Organizational psychotherapy proceeds on the basis that the collective psyche of an organization is similar in nature to the psyche of the individual and is similarly amenable to therapeutic interventions (although the actual techniques and underlying concepts may differ). With the focus on relationship building, communication, conflict resolution, and behavior change, organizational psychotherapy can improve an organization's well-being and overall effectiveness, extending to external stakeholders such as customers and partners/suppliers.

Organizational psychotherapists are becoming more and more common. So much so that the concept appears in mainstream television now. Currently, there is a television program called *Billions* that features a character by the name of Wendy Rhoades. Wendy plays a resident psychiatrist for Axe Capital, a hedge fund company. Although Rhoades is a psychiatrist, she is often referred to as the company's "performance coach," lending an ear to employees who need to vent, discussing strategies to improve performance, and giving advice to employees that need counsel to deal with their emotional stress. Calling her a "performance coach" versus a "psychiatrist" is a topic for another day, but let's just say it has everything to do with the stigma attached to therapy. As that stigma decreases, there may be a growing movement for organizations to incorporate resident psychotherapists. The television show highlights power, greed, egoism, and the pursuit of justice, so you can imagine there are a lot of opportunities to explore the psyches of the individuals involved.

More and more companies these days are making holistic commitments to employee well-being, and this absolutely includes an employee's psychological health. At the Wellbeing@Work conference in 2017, a CEO and co-founder of a very successful firm that specializes in workplace psychotherapy said, "In 5 years, you are going to see therapy offered to employees at every major employer across the country as a vital service to enhance productivity. How do I know this? Because we're seeing it already."[10]

For example, Certified Angus Beef, a 125-employee Ohio company, offers in-house therapy to employees twice a month at no cost and on company time. The "perk" shows the employees that they are valued, and it helps to reduce the overall stigma surrounding mental health and therapy. A commitment to mental health has become part of their workplace culture. The company's human resources director reportedly said, "We want our employees to be healthy and happy and engaged and challenged

---

10   Erin Frey, "The New Frontier—Therapy in the Workplace," Medium, July 12, 2017, https://medium.com/kip-blog/the-new-frontier-therapy-in-the-workplace-aadb91735628.

and motivated."[11] As a result of the in-house therapy and a few other health and wellness initiatives (access to fitness classes and meditation, free legal services, and others), the company enjoys a very minimal turnover rate—3 percent, which is much lower than the industry average of 10 percent.

Although organizational psychotherapy (OP) may overlap with other specializations of business psychologies such as industrial and organizational (IO) psychology or organization development (OD), they are not similar in their approaches. For example, IO psychology may specifically address employee selection or training and development, while OD may focus on change management, workflow, or policies and procedures. All three specialties—OP, OD, and IO—focus on application in the organizational setting, but the approach from these perspectives are different.

The Government's Role in Capitalism

The attempts to address the effects of unscrupulous individuals in business are changing, and companies are not the only ones taking initiative. The government has also stepped in to try to strengthen the system. Whether or not financial collapse was caused by an unstable free market system or a few bad apples, the response from the government was to make efforts to hold businesses accountable through regulation and reform. Three historical examples of government intervention after corporate fraud include the Security and Exchange Commission (SEC) of 1934, the Sarbanes-Oxley Act (SOX) of 2002, and the Corporate Fraud Task Force (CFTF) established in 2002.

In 2009, President Barack Obama expanded the CFTF and renamed it the Interagency Financial Fraud Enforcement Task Force to strengthen efforts to combat financial crime. The continued expansion of government corporate oversight signals that corporate fraud may be more evident than we anticipated.

---

11   Emily Peck, "This Small Company Offers On-Site Therapy to Workers," *Huffington Post*, January 12, 2016, https://www.huffpost.com/entry/certified-angus-beef-therapy_n _56707e76e4b011b83a6d0755.

However well-intentioned government regulations may be, they are a Band-Aid on a gunshot wound. Federal regulations are not enough to change the result because change needs to come from the bottom up, from the people that make up the system, the people, that is. The root issue needs to be addressed, which is a rethinking of the way we all interact with companies, conduct our own businesses, and conceive of the economic system itself. We essentially need to renegotiate the social contract of capitalism.

As the world slipped into economic meltdown after the 2008 financial crisis, the nation revived fervent talks about greed: greedy lenders, greedy Wall Street executives, greedy CEOs, and greedy Americans who used credit to finance unattainable lifestyles.

Capitalism is our economic system because it is supposed to put the power in the hands of the people. We hold and harness the power to innovate and collaborate. We have the power to positively impact society, take care of ourselves and our families, and create value for new and unique goods and services. We have the power to choose what we buy and what we don't buy. We also have the power to change the system. Just as we work to heal our own psyches when things go awry, we have the power to heal the system by adjusting our intention, our expectations, our motivations, and our overall approach to this system that impacts us on each level of our existence. In this context, a more conscious approach to capitalism can be one clue as to what we can do about our relationship with capitalism.

CHAPTER SEVEN

THE RISE OF CONSCIOUSNESS

When consciousness guides our mental
facilities, the result can be brilliant.

–Patricia Aburdene[12]

"You've had a lot of time to think about the context of your concerns and about your history," I told Capitalism the next time we met. "We've talked about what happens when there is dysfunction. Have you stumbled upon any actions you can take to improve your sense of self?"

"I've been thinking about it a lot," my patient told me. "But I don't think you're going to like the answer."

Now I was intrigued. "Oh?"

"Well, you said something during our last session, about how systems are made up of people. And that's just the thing, isn't it? Dysfunction comes in part from others. But I do see some positive signs."

"Let's talk about those," I said, hoping to steer my patient toward productive ideas.

"Customers today have a different relationship with me and with businesses. Instead of being spoon-fed advertisements, they can get real-time information and share their own experiences. Customers are also more educated about marketing and business. Conscious Capitalism is on the rise, and women are shaping business in some promising ways. I'm feeling optimistic."

---

12 Patricia Aburdene, *Megatrends 2010* (Newburyport, MA: Hampton Roads Publishing Company, 2005), xvi.

For the rest of the session, Capitalism and I spoke about the positive steps he was seeing in the world. As soon as he left, I completed my clinical note for the session and then opened my journal to capture my own reflections.

It's not unusual for families to come to me with specific ideas of the "problem" and where it comes from. "My husband just ignores me," a partner may say. "My parents don't understand me," a child may claim.

One of the first steps we take together, after taking patient histories and evaluating the problem, is to get conscious about the situation.

Put plainly, the concept of consciousness is a person's level of awareness, alertness, and mindfulness. It is also the ability to experience reality while being aware of others and how our actions impact them, and being keenly aware of one's inner values and applying those values to the outside world.

When a spouse becomes aware their partner is having trouble at work or is struggling with another problem, that shifts their awareness from "he's the problem" to a shared issue they can work on together. Consciousness paves the way for a common approach together.

When we each expand our worldview and lifestyle in this way—when we are conscious—we feel more connected to others, more whole, and more fulfilled. The result of this strong sense of belonging and worth is personal growth and, ultimately, collective growth.

"Consciousness" and "social interest" are interrelated concepts. One cannot have healthy levels of social interest without being conscious. After all, consciousness is the foundation of social interest. We must be aware of ourselves, our inner drives, and how we impact others. Once we acknowledge that we affect others, we feel a sense of connection and belonging in a community.

As a psychotherapist, when I use an Adlerian lens, I evaluate a person's level of social interest, help them become aware of that value set within themselves, and help them grow it. One cannot grow social interest until there is an acute awareness, or consciousness, of inner goals, values, and motivations. Part of growing social interest involves developing empathy, positive attitudes toward others, and concern for others' well-being—all things that require being conscious.

It does not just happen at a personal level, either. There has been a substantial growth in individual *and* collective consciousness in the world. We see this in the concern communities and individuals show about the impact we have on the environment and in a greater awareness of the many peoples and cultures across the globe. We also see this in the way younger job candidates look for jobs that make a difference, not just a salary.

Raj Sisodia, one of the founders of the Conscious Capitalism movement, believes this shift in collective consciousness to be a result of technological advances, an aging population, and a growing prevalence of feminine values.

Let's take a look at that first factor. The world has been forever changed by the advent of the internet. Patricia Aburdene, a social forecaster and leader in the Conscious Capitalism movement, said that technology is consciousness externalized. The internet has allowed for technological advances in communication tools that give us the opportunity to communicate more frequently and from greater distances compared to the earlier parts of the twentieth century. We can chat with people in all corners of the world instantly. Gone are the days where we had to rely on the media or a long trip through the postal service to learn about what is going on in other parts of the world. We are more connected now than ever before.

The introduction of social media heightened this sense of togetherness among the global community. Online social networks have been the catalysts for political demonstrations, and human rights protests, and, on a smaller scale, have allowed us to stay connected with friends and family while introducing new connections we would have never made.

Although there are arguments surrounding the internet and social media's effect on traditional connections and relationships, the benefits of being knowledgeable about what is taking place halfway around the world are immeasurable. In 2011, a revolution in Tunisia was amplified via social media, and that charge spread to multiple other countries—this revolution is known as the Arab Spring. If it weren't for social media and internet access, those protests and subsequent demonstrations would have never been known on a global scale.

Since the introduction of the internet, we have quick and easy access to limitless information. When I was a child, I had to go to the library and consult enormous sets of thick books called encyclopedias (the predecessor of Wikipedia, for those who don't know) to research or write a report. Hours and hours were spent in libraries poring over heavy books searching for the information I needed. Oftentimes, my library wouldn't have the books I needed, and I would have to either go to another library or wait for that book to be mailed to my library in order to finish my research. Thinking back on how cumbersome and painstaking the process was to even write a simple school report, I am very appreciative of the easy access to the limitless information online today. A quick Google search now gives us information instantly. This free and immediate access to so much information has the potential to make us a more intelligent, better informed, and more educated society.

This access to information and to communication online affects consciousness in a few ways. We can read blogs and news reports from around the world, learning about the cultures and daily lives of people who live far from us. The immediacy of being able to read first-hand accounts of situations we might not otherwise hear about can make us feel connected and curious about others as well as better informed, which in turn can increase our consciousness and our social interest.

This digital revolution has also resulted in unprecedented transparency in government and business. Businesses are now held accountable in ways they never were before. Many companies are now required to openly share their financial information online, along with other pertinent details of operations.

Perhaps one of the more compelling outcomes of the digital revolution is the shift of power from the company to the consumer. Gone are the days of one-way communication from business to consumer, wherein the passive customer was served highly controlled messages and cherry-picked details about a company's behavior.

Consumers are no longer passive, and they have the power to play an active role in capitalism by researching, inquiring, and demanding truthful information about products and services. When social media came into the forefront, it created a new landscape for consumers and businesses alike. Consumers can share opinions of companies with unparalleled speed, freedom, and reach. From Yelp and TripAdvisor to Facebook and Twitter (and many more social tools out there), consumers have a built-in audience of millions to read their opinion on a company, product, or service. It is harder for companies to hide bad customer service or poor products, for example, when consumers are able to easily and instantly share information about companies online.

For example, United Airlines was caught in the crosshairs of this situation in 2017 when a passenger released a cell phone video of an incident on one of the flights. The airline had overbooked their flight, and it had been their policy in those cases to mandate that a randomly assigned passenger be bumped off the flight. Things became ugly onboard as the passenger they were looking to bump was adamantly not giving up the seat he paid for. The passenger was a doctor on his way to Kentucky, and it was essential for him to see his patients the next morning. The situation spiraled out of control when airport security boarded the plane and physically dragged him off, bloodying his face in the process. This disturbing scene was caught on tape by another passenger and uploaded to Facebook. The immediate, and deserved, backlash against United quickly ensued. The horrible mismanagement of the overbooked flight situation was the beginning of the problem, but hours after the onboard tussle stunned passengers, the public was enraged. Any good will that United had built over many years of decent customer service and millions of dollars in marketing quickly evaporated. It wasn't long before the airline that bore the tagline "fly the friendly skies" was ruined in a disastrous public relations crisis that they have yet to recover from.

Companies must act like everyone is watching, because they are. This spotlight on civility necessitates both companies and customers to engage in solution-focused, problem-solving dialogue.

Businesses have new platforms to consumers as well. They can target consumers based on a variety of characteristics, from demographics to on-line behavior. This will be talked about in more detail later in the book. The main point here is the way that the internet and social media have opened up communications and made us more aware of, well . . . everything.

The research I completed and which I detailed at the start of this book addresses this two-way communication, wherein companies like Google and eBay are able to communicate their marketing messages but where consumers take an active role in interpreting that data. In some cases, consumers interpret the data in ways the company did not intend, and businesses need to strive to do better. The increased transparency puts pressure on companies to not just communicate differently but also to behave differently.

At the same time as this technological shift is taking place, there is a related shift in how people approach their lives.

Statistics show that as a society, we place a higher value on our life's purpose, meaning, and connectedness than we have in the past. The number one thing college graduates are looking for in a job is to feel that they are contributing to something bigger than themselves.

In my practice, I counsel people of various socioeconomic levels. Even some of the wealthier patients that I have worked with were unsatisfied because they found their high-paying job to be dull and unfulfilling. Despite their six-figure earnings, they talked about the possibility of changing careers, or doing something to fulfill their need to contribute to society in a meaningful way—a clear movement toward social interest.

I recall one patient in particular (we'll call her Rayna). She was a pharmacist who had worked for ten years, only having to work three days a week dispensing medication. For Rayna, being a pharmacist paid handsomely, but it did not provide a sense of belonging or meaningfulness.

After listening to her complaints about how much she hated her job, I asked Rayna why. She said, "It's boring. I'm on my feet ten hours a day, my posture is not right because of it, and I don't even believe the medications that I am giving people will help them. I feel stuck."

The job she was doing was not congruent with her own beliefs. Consequently, she came to therapy to attempt to resolve this inner conflict. Little did she know, she was already steps ahead of others on her road to being aware of the root of her conflict and, therefore, able to make a change in her life. Her consciousness of the inner struggle helped her make a career change more easily than those who are not yet aware of why they are unsatisfied.

Psychotherapy helps people become conscious of their inner selves and reeducate themselves on how to interpret their feelings and motivations. I remember watching Howard Stern, the most widely known American radio and television personality, on a talk show once. I believe it was David Letterman's *My Next Guest Needs No Introduction*. In the interview, Stern praised his involvement with psychotherapy and talked about his journey toward self-awareness.

"I think I did a lot of growing up, and I do attribute this to psychotherapy," Stern said. "I was just a young man full of rage. I could not love anyone. I could not respect anyone. I just thought this was who I was. [There was] a lack of self-examination. It was through psychotherapy that I started to fall in love with life a little bit. I started to appreciate what was good."

Howard Stern was expressing his movement toward greater consciousness and higher social interest. For him, as for so many of my patients, the two are intertwined.

Consciousness and awareness allows us to reexamine, explore, and evaluate where we are, where we want to go, and who we want to be. When we are conscious, we can ask ourselves, "How do I want to be involved with and contribute to the outside world, the greater good? What does being in this world look like?" It is vital that we are aware of our valued place in this world and can identify what matters most to us.

People want to feel that their jobs have purpose beyond a paycheck. Being more conscious, we are more aware of our impact on our relationships, our families, and our planet. This consciousness has, in turn, affected our levels of social interest and resulted in a global society that has journeyed to a level of connectedness like never before.

In the late 1980s, for the first time in recorded history, the median age of the population was over forty. Generally speaking, when someone reaches this age, they often have a family and others in their life that naturally forces a shift in inner values. Younger people tend to be most concerned with their own health and well-being, while older people tend to place a higher value on caring, concern for others, nurturing, life meaning, and a higher purpose.

There are still incidents of the stereotypical "mid-life crisis" wherein which a person overcompensates for those values and engages in an often-short-lived moment of self-centeredness. However, for the most part, people entering middle age tend to value tradition and meaning in life. This focus on meaning and a higher purpose amplifies the rise of our collective consciousness.

The rise of women in education and in the workplace has also contributed to our collective shift on account of the influence of "feminine" values. There are more women in college than there are men. More businesses today are started by women than men. Feminine values include empathy, selflessness, collaboration, patience, and caring (note that these are also values shared by the definition of social interest). However, feminine values don't solely belong to women. Leaders of both genders can embrace feminine values, and research has shown that approaching business with dominant feminine values positively impacts the global economy and social well-being.

John Gerzema, a pioneer in the use of data to identify social change and help companies anticipate and adapt to new interests and demands, and Michael D'Antonio, a celebrated author and Pulitzer Prize-winning journalist, wrote about feminine values in their book *The Athena Doctrine: How Women (and the Men That Think Like Them) Will Rule the World*. Their vast study proved that we live in a world that's increasingly social, interdependent, and transparent. And in this world, feminine values are ascendant. Their survey of sixty-four thousand people from around the world showed that traditionally feminine leadership and values are now more popular than the "macho" paradigm of the past.

The most innovative leaders among us are breaking away from traditional structures to be more flexible, collaborative, and nurturing. And both men and women all over the globe are adopting this style. All over the world, people are deploying feminine thinking and values to make their lives, and the world, better.

Our inner values shape our actions, and as we have evolved into a more conscious society, we also have the capital power to invest our hard-earned money in products and businesses that align with our values. Studies show that consumers are motivated to use their buying power with companies whose mission, purpose, and values are similar to their own. This forces businesses to take a long, hard look at their own philosophies and behaviors. Businesses are operating in a theoretical glass house at this point and must be authentic in their founding philosophies and practices.

Changing the Story

When we get conscious, something else happens: we start telling a different internal story. For example, when a patient comes to me to say their partner "does not care," she may use examples to support that story: "Oh, he never mows the lawn," or "She's always asking me to do things instead of helping."

When a couple or individual gets conscious about this process and about their role, their internal story can shift as well. When we open our eyes and take stock, we allow ourselves to step out of the loop we've created. Instead of using new facts to feed the same old story, we can create a new one: "Maybe he isn't mowing the lawn because he is tried or because I have not asked."

By getting conscious about capitalism, we create a new story. Instead of sweeping statements such as "capitalism is bad" or "capitalism hurts people," we can dive deeper and get specific. We can ask ourselves, "Why do some people act badly within the framework of capitalism? How can I support more businesses to act consciously? How can I be part of the shift to create the type of capitalism I want?"

We are collectively awakening and have the power to amend our economic system to align with our needs and values. We are entering the era of Conscious Capitalism.

But of course it's not enough to know something is wrong. We also have to be willing to act on what we learn. If a couple in crisis came to me, I would help to deescalate the crisis and then give them homework or tasks to work on together so that they can improve their problem-solving and ultimately strengthen their relationship. What can I prescribe in this case?

CHAPTER EIGHT

CONSCIOUS BUSINESS

Many of the problems in the world today remain unresolved because we continue to interpret capitalism too narrowly.

−Muhammad Yunus[13]

When Capitalism walked into my office the next time, he was a changed person. He walked taller and was wearing a new suit.

Capitalism smiled, looking more relaxed than he had been in a while. "I've learned a lot from you. Adler would be proud with the social interest and all. And I've realized a few things."

I was intrigued. "Oh?"

"Yeah. I'm changing, is what you helped me realize. This whole technology and internet thing is changing me more than I realize. People have a more intimate relationship with businesses, and it is changing my relationship with people. They expect more of businesses—and of me. I need to accept that I'm changing and my relationships are changing. I need to step up to the plate."

"How do you plan on doing that?"

Capitalism winked. "Well, I've decided to take some time to travel. I've changed, and the world has changed. I want to explore what that looks like and discover more about myself."

---

13   Muhammad Yunus, "Social Business Entrepreneurs are the Solution," in *Humanism in Business*, ed. Heiko Spitzeck, Wolfgang Amann, Michael Pirson, Shiban Khan, and Ernst von Kimakowitz (New York: Cambridge University Press, 2009), 402.

Capitalism leaped off the coach, shook my hand again, and headed out. And with that, Capitalism walked out of my office for the last time, as abruptly as he had first arrived.

Stunned, I blinked at the empty couch for some time. I thought back over our many sessions and the journal I had started. I thought about my dissertation and considered all I had explored and considered. I really had been learning all along, shifting my relationship with one of the biggest systems in my life.

Smiling now, I returned to my journal. Inspired and passionate, I found the words flowed out of me.

It is time for a new interpretation of capitalism, one that aims at collaboration over competition. This is a paradigm shift from individualistic thinking to a more generous social mantra founded in the principle that capitalism is much more than a profit-making system. It reaches far beyond a mutually beneficial transaction and greatly impacts all stakeholders in the system.

It's not only time for a new interpretation for capitalism, but it appears that changes are occurring to change the way we think about business. As we saw in my own survey, customers are actively thinking about companies not just as providers of services and products but as more holistic parts of the society. Consumers are aware of and care about what companies do and what they stand for.

Conscious Capitalism champion Patricia Aburdene said in her book *Megatrends 2010: The Rise of Conscious Capitalism* that the spirituality movement is the greatest megatrend of our era, and the spiritual transformation is now spilling over from the personal to the institutional. Spiritual trends are transforming the way people consume and the way entrepreneurs do business. The term "spiritual" in this context can be interchanged with "consciousness," "mindfulness," or "awareness."

Citizens are becoming more aware and conscious about their inner values and are more eager to do business with companies that share those values. For example, I have a friend who will only purchase products that are made in the United States. My cousin will only buy coffee that is free-trade certified. My wife is strongly against purchasing anything packaged in nonrecycled or nonrecyclable plastic. All of these overt purchase behaviors have a real impact on businesses.

At the same time, businesses are recognizing the emergence of values-driven consumers and their demands for companies to treat people, communities, and the environment in a more meaningful way. Caring for the mental and physical health of employees is mandatory if an employer wants to attract and retain employees. Not all businesses can provide on-site massage therapists, on-campus gyms, and/or free childcare, but companies are becoming more and more aware of the necessity to holistically care for their employees and stakeholders.

Given this surge of consciousness, both consumers and businesses are searching for ways to align their values and purposes and finding ways to coexist. The next step is to redefine the existing social contract between businesses and consumers.

A social contract is an understanding or agreement between individuals or groups that is meant to ensure mutual benefit. The contract that we've had with traditional capitalism may have reached a point where it is no longer mutually beneficial, or maybe it needs some additional checks and balances incorporated within the agreement to meet the needs of all parties.

New Business Models

No matter how you approach the system, the players remain the same. There are employees, leaders, investors, vendors and supply chains, customers, the environment, and others all working together in the system. What distinguishes people most in terms of approach is whether you see the system with a shareholder-centric approach or a stakeholder-centric approach. Shareholders are individuals who invest in a business and have a financial stake or share in the corporation. These are the venture capitalists, the investment firms, the people who own stock in a company.

For decades, the corporate landscape has been dominated by business models that prioritize profit and shareholder value over all else. However, more businesses are now concerned with creating value for all of their stakeholders (including customers, employees, supply chain, environment, and investors). The Sustainable Enterprise Economy (SEE) describes it as a broad movement of companies emerging as "business unusual." Business unusual refers to for-profit corporations that integrate prosocial goals into their very essence. The benefit corporation, B Corps, and Conscious Capitalism are three examples of recently defined formal business structures that build philosophies and practices around prosocial goals.

Benefit corporations are state-registered "triple bottom line" (people, planet, and profit) businesses that are legally created to focus on more than just maximizing shareholder profits. Traditional corporations risk being sued if they don't prioritize shareholder profit, but registration as a benefit corporation allows for a business structure that provides the legal protection for a company to pursue social and/or environmental goals as well as increasing shareholder profit.

Similar in name to the benefit corporation is the "B Corp." A Certified B Corp business strives to meet the highest standards of verified social and environmental performance, public transparency, and legal accountability to balance profit and purpose. The "B" stands for "benefit" and refers to benefiting workers, the community, and the environment. B Corps are certified by the nonprofit organization B Lab, which assesses and audits companies to ensure that they follow through on their claims. This is similar to the way that TransFair certifies fair-trade coffee, or the way the USDA certifies organic food. B Lab has certified several thousand companies around the world and provides a global standard and stamp of approval for benefit-minded corporations. Kleen Kanteen, the first environmentally friendly, reusable bottle created free of BPA and other dangerous toxins, is a B Corp.

The differences in benefit corporations and B Corps can be explained by their status as registered or certified entities. As previously stated, benefit corporations are state "registered," affording them the legal protection to not only pursue profit but also address people and the planet. B Corps, on the other hand, are "certified" and are not legally protected from shareholders, who may be unsatisfied with the business's multiple motivations. A company can be registered as either or both a benefit corporation (if a state allows it) and/or certified as a B Corp. Patagonia, whose mission is to "Build the best product, cause no unnecessary harm, use business to inspire and implement solutions to the environmental crisis," is both a benefit corporation and a B Corp. Now we can all agree that the forty-year-old global company is likely making a profit for its investors, but it continues to prove to be committed to its mission.

The designations of both benefit corporation and B Corp also provides accountability and responsibility for efforts toward social and environmental responsibility. There are certainly companies that claim to be "sustainable," "green," or "give back," but if a company has not been certified, those are often simply empty claims used as marketing tactics—some call it "greenwashing."

I am the father of a young toddler, so I have done my fair share of researching what products are safest to use with my daughter. In 2009,

Huggies put out a new line of diapers and called it "Pure and Natural." By the next year, I was reading that the only thing natural about their new product line was an organic cotton exterior. The rest of the diaper was exactly the same as any other disposable diaper on the market, right down to the petrochemical gel on the inside. Several publications called out the company for greenwashing. These types of deceptive marketing are just ploys and have nothing to do with the stated philosophies or mission of a company.

Times are changing the way people and businesses interact. In order for a company to connect with consumers and retain a vibrant workforce, it must be mindful and conscious. John Mackey is one of the cofounders of the Conscious Capitalism movement and cofounder and CEO of Whole Foods Market. He also coauthored what I consider the "bible" of Conscious Capitalism, the bestselling book *Conscious Capitalism: Liberating the Heroic Spirit of Business*.

Mackey defines Conscious Capitalism as an interdependent ecosystem of conscious businesses interacting with each other. Again, we are talking about an overarching system within which conscious businesses (benefit corporations, B Corps, and others who embody a conscious business model) operate. Conscious business is a more spiritual and enlightened approach to business that forces leaders to analyze and potentially refocus the real purpose of their existence.

Just as Mackey described companies seeking a higher purpose, we can see customers and patients striving for significance.

In fact, people naturally strive toward significance. They want to feel a sense of belonging. Included in this search for meaningfulness is a self-exploration of one's purpose or passion.

Yet while people want to pursue their passion, they also face fears. One of the challenges I hear when I work with potential entrepreneurs is the hesitation to follow their dreams due to the usual "risk-taking" involved in the process. There's a sense of uncertainty, a lack of control over outcomes, and a fear of failure. I have found myself engaging these patients in the process of identifying their life purpose. Once this is identified, I work with them in improving their confidence in taking decisive actions so they can get their greatest work into the world.

Once patients are able to overcome their uncertainty, I've noticed that their happiness is found when they are able to provide a service that helps others. When they focus on the people they serve instead of focusing on themselves: social interest!

As my patients focus more on others, they sometimes even gain confidence in pursuing their purpose. An author who wants to write for fame may get stuck, but an author who decides to write children's books so children can sleep at night and have awesome dreams is no longer focused on self. This external focus can make it easier for the writer to connect with his or her audience.

It is similar with business.

As businesses focus on customers and stakeholders rather than the narrower goal of self-interest or profits, they are able to connect with customers and create a passion-driven purpose that motivates employees. Is it any wonder such companies are growing and companies are embracing the Conscious Capitalism message? As more and more businesses practice consciously, I predict our market will reach a tipping point where traditional capitalism will be replaced by Conscious Capitalism.

Conscious Capitalism is already rapidly growing in its membership as it continues to be pioneered by leading executives in the business and academic worlds, including, but not limited to: Howard Behar, formerly of Starbucks; Daniel Lubetzky, of KIND; Denise Morrison, formerly of Campbell Soup; Melissa Reiff, of the Container Store; Ron Shaich, of Panera Bread; and Jostein Solheim, of Ben & Jerry's. Books, journals, and media have continued to inform the masses of how Conscious Capitalism can humanize the workplace, create value and meaning, and make a difference in the world.

As a response to the public mistrust of business, and businesses' desire to restore consumer confidence, the idea of Conscious Capitalism has come at a time when the world needs it the most. Businesses have realized that they have a responsibility to humankind—their customers and those who keep them in business—to align with societal values and to rebuild the relationship that has been weakened by rampant corporate greed. The fact that customers react favorably to Conscious Capitalism companies and such companies profit while fulfilling their purpose just adds more momentum to the movement.

Principles of Conscious Capitalism

Conscious Capitalism has four fundamental mutually reinforcing principles:

Purpose. The first principle of conscious business is pursuing a higher purpose above simple profits. Conscious businesses have a deeper purpose beyond maximizing profits and shareholder value. Many in the traditional capitalism school of thought believe that a company's principal goal is financial gain, and thus there is an ultimate commitment to shareholders—the people with a financial stake in the company. Conscious companies still make a profit and are concerned with profit, but they also ask about the contributions they can make to stakeholders, their community, and the world.

Milton Friedman (1912–2006), still taught in business schools today, purports that business's sole purpose is to generate profit for shareholders. Friedman's teachings align with the Shareholder Wealth Maximization (SWM) approach to business, which posits that profit generation was not only the ultimate purpose of business but also the chief operating goal. The popular mantra that business's primary goal is to make profit has been taught and justified by business schools and business professionals for decades. In fact, the literature in the disciplines of economics and finance still define SWM as a "standard practice."

However, profit as the sole purpose of business can encourage short-term thinking and can result in corporations treating people and the natural environment as instruments for profit-making. This approach effectively results in businesses disregarding the social, moral, and relational aspects of life (the same factors that lead to low social interest, and we know how that impacts the health of an individual and a system). Meanwhile, it is these ignored factors that are what ultimately contribute to the health and long-term success of a business.

This more holistic approach to the purpose of a business is preferred and supported by some of the most respected business minds today.

The emerging paradigm of Conscious Capitalism refutes the SWM approach and argues that businesses need a deeper purpose that transcends profits. Profit still matters, but it should not be the sole purpose of a business. Conscious businesses believe that pursuing a higher purpose should be the priority. In this sense, the mission and reason for being becomes a more intrinsic motivator that engenders passion, sustained engagement, and value within and outside the company. Compare that to a rather simplistic idea that incentive and inspiration comes solely from profit chasing.

Conscious consumers have become more apt to buy from a company that is mindful of the community, the environment, and other causes of social justice. Conscious or values-driven consumers account for a growing $250 billion market.

Furthermore, employees are working and aligning themselves with businesses that fit their values and add meaning and worth to their lives. Having a higher purpose makes employees feel emotionally engaged, inspires them, and gives them a sense of purpose. Conscious businesses have a higher purpose that institutionalize an ethical commitment to all stakeholders, including, but not limited to, consumers, employees, and the community.

Examples of companies that incorporate a higher purpose in their practices include Disney, Johnson & Johnson, Southwest Airlines, and BMW. Disney's higher purpose is to use their imagination to bring happiness to millions. Southwest Airlines' purpose is to give people the freedom to fly, and BMW's higher purpose is to enable people to experience the joy of driving.

Stakeholder Orientation. Research has shown that cooperation is more effective and efficient than competition. Competition often distracts, creates anxiety, and is consequently a barrier to success. Managing a conscious business involves efforts to create synergistic harmonies and produce win-win-win scenarios for all stakeholders while refraining from exploitation or trade-offs. Conscious Capitalism accomplishes this through a stakeholder orientation, which rivals the more widely practiced shareholder orientation that we just discussed.

Remember that a shareholder orientation approach to business advances the notion that the sole goal of a corporation is to maximize profits for its investors and owners. Businesses that operate with a shareholder orientation most likely hold a zero-sum view of business, which is intrinsically competitive.

A zero-sum mentality is a term used in community psychology to describe a way of thinking that hangs on the notion that there must always be one winner and one loser. In this sense, shareholders win and other stakeholder groups lose. Many of the proponents of the traditional shareholder orientation argue that it is impossible for all constituents in a stakeholder orientation to have equal interests since all interests seem to contradict each other, which ultimately results in trade-offs and exploitation.

In contrast, leaders of conscious businesses view their companies as holistic institutions that are impacted by all participants involved. Similar to a person with a high level of social interest, they are aware of their goals and aim for a higher purpose, a sense of belonging, and a strong desire to contribute to the common good. Conscious businesses operate with an understanding of the significant role that all stakeholder groups play in the organization, valuing all of their constituents equally. "Stakeholders" in a business can be defined as any individual, group, or organization that has an interest in the corporation: investors, employees, vendors, the community, and customers. Conscious business leaders value all stakeholders equally and thus work to balance the stakeholders' interests with an aim of creating value and fairness among all of the constituents.

The central theme in the stakeholder perspective of conscious businesses is the value and recognition of the total interdependence between all stakeholders. The inherent interconnectedness of stakeholder groups requires them to work together and to meet goals that are often aligned. This collaboration in turn creates value, synergies, and connectedness within the organizational system. A profitable and sustainable business can be built from this cooperation. In this way, conscious businesses are able to manage not only profitability but, more importantly, responsibility to all their stakeholders, including the planet and the community. Hence, the practice of stakeholder orientation has shifted how business leaders think and marks how Conscious Capitalism is distinct from other economic paradigms.

Conscious Leadership. In order for a business to be conscious, it must have conscious leadership. Conscious leaders are considered highly analytical, emotional, and spiritual, and have world-centric perspectives that have helped them create conscious business cultures. Their thinking does not focus on differences, conflicts, trade-offs, and zero-sum situations but on the possibility of a win-win in every situation. Being socially responsible in business requires that leaders feel, think, and act in ways that consider and address the global economy and global social factors.

If the individuals in power are psychologically healthy and have a high level of social interest, they will have a propensity to be naturally concerned with the health and well-being of everyone involved. Therefore, how a leader encourages, develops, respects, and positively impacts others should be the priority focus when studying leadership qualities. While much literature about leadership focuses on skills, psychology and emotional health are just as crucial, if not more so, for conscious leadership.

Conscious leaders are aware of the consequences of their actions and how they will ultimately impact and create value for all stakeholders. A conscious leader adheres to a higher purpose and has a stakeholder-oriented mode of operation and thinking. Thus, a conscious leader incorporates the first two tenets of Conscious Capitalism and exemplifies the third tenet by basing their leadership philosophies on the Servant Leadership Theory.

While servant leadership is a timeless concept, the phrase "servant leadership" was coined by Robert K. Greenleaf in "The Servant as Leader," an essay that he first published in 1970. Servant Leadership Theory is based on Greenleaf's model of making others, including employees, customers, and community, the number one priority. This theory of leadership has gained prominence in many organizations. Craig Johnson, a leader in organizational ethics and leaders, wrote in his book *Meeting the Ethical Challenges of Leadership: Casting Light or Shadow*, "The advantages of the servant leadership model are its altruism, simplicity, and self-awareness. It emphasizes the moral sense of concern for others, reducing the complexity engendered by putting personal desires in conflict with those of followers."[14]

Servant leaders are conscious of their role in the organization. They help employees achieve through support, inspiration, education, praise, coaching, and listening. Servant leaders continuously want to make a difference with the people they work with and at the same time impact the organization. They leave their egos behind and understand how they should work together with others to implement vision and motivate others to

---

14   Craig E. Johnson, *Meeting the Ethical Challenges of Leadership: Casting Light or Shadow*, sixth edition (Thousand Oaks, CA: Sage Publishing, 2011), 270.

thrive. These leadership traits are very similar to those that are considered "feminine" leadership values.

Conscious Culture. Society as a whole is becoming more conscious, mindful, or "spiritual." The convergence between spiritually driven individuals and the corporate social responsibility movement has sparked a transformation in business. Company cultures are transforming because people are becoming more intentional about goals, purpose, and values.

When a company exemplifies the first three tenets of Conscious Capitalism—Purpose, Stakeholder Orientation, and Conscious Leadership—the company will likely have a culture of consciousness.

Organizational culture has been defined as a general system of rules that governs meanings in organization. Conscious cultures create an environment of purposeful, meaningful, and ethical action. The best way to describe a conscious organizational culture is by using the acronym TACTILE, which stands for trust, authenticity, caring, transparency, integrity, learning, and empowerment. Conscious cultures incorporate ethics, social responsibility, and sustainability practices into core practices. This strategy of integration makes it more likely that these values are inherent and practiced on a consistent basis within the work culture.

Conscious Capitalism versus Corporate Social Responsibility

Many assume that businesses that practice corporate social responsibility (CSR) are the same as conscious businesses. The differences between CSR and Conscious Capitalism can be explained by comparing their respective business models. Most companies that practice CSR are simply adding social responsibility to their operations while potentially keeping a profit-driven business model that is most concerned with shareholder results. This is the term used to describe when a company boasts its social responsibility commitments but fails to embed those elements into its core philosophies and approach to business.

A conscious business, on the other hand, prioritizes a higher purpose and takes into account all stakeholders. Because conscious business models identify society and the environment as stakeholders, they have a responsibility to then address societal and environmental issues. Because these responsibilities are embedded into the culture, conscious businesses are clearly and genuinely communicating the higher purpose of the business.

Operational Values of Conscious Businesses

An operational value is an observable or measurable factor that contributes to an end state. Imagine you are trying to get healthy. In order to reach your goal, you need to get better rest, get to a healthy weight, eat more whole foods, and start moving more. You may walk one mile every other day or go to spin class three times a week to reach your goal. You may start including vegetables with every meal and save dessert for special occasions. Those measurable and observable actions—the number of spin classes each week, hours slept per night, or miles ran—are the operational values of the system that will get you to your end state, getting healthier.

This works in therapy, too, though it can seem counterintuitive to measure in the same way. If a couple wants to strengthen their relationship, they may have to define what success will look like. Perhaps that would mean measuring how happy they are with their relationship on a scale of 1 to 10. To strengthen their relationship, they may decide to have one meaningful conversation a day and one date a week.

There are also observable and measurable things that businesses have or do that determine whether the company is conscious. When a business has low employee turnover and high employee morale, gives exceptional experiences to its customers, has loyal customer bases, exemplifies humanitarian and environmental involvement, and prioritizes stakeholder interconnectedness and interdependence, the business is most likely operating from a conscious business orientation. We can even say a company with these attributes is healthy and operating with high social interest.

The valued employee. Conscious businesses value a meaningful workplace for their employees. They recognize that employees should feel valued and cared for, which results in low employee turnover and high employee morale. Conscious businesses show they value their employees by investing time, effort, and money on their unique selection, training, and retention practices.

Conscious businesses hire employees that align with their organizational values and unique passions. Hiring for organizational fit leads to the hiring of intrinsically motivated employees who genuinely find their work enjoyable and meaningful.

Conscious businesses also provide extensive training that is much more than the average training period. For example, The Container Store requires more than twenty times more hours of training than the average retail store. Some conscious businesses, such as Southwest Airlines and Commerce Bank, have developed their own universities to train their employees, while others offer continuous training, educational and advancement opportunities, and mentorship.

Because conscious businesses value their employees and are committed to a culture that embraces meaning, purpose, a sense of belonging, and education, it should come as no surprise that employees tend to stay. For example, The Container Store reports that their turnover is more than ten times less than the turnover in similar industries, and Starbucks has a turnover rate that is 250 percent lower than the industry average. Likewise, conscious businesses such as Whole Foods Market, Costco, Southwest Airlines, and Wegmans all have a significantly lower employee turnover rate compared to other companies in similar industries.

Conscious businesses believe that workplaces don't have to be dreaded or feared. Instead, they try to create workplaces that are fun and enthusiastic, where each employee can be authentic and where cooperation as a team is encouraged. These values result in high employee morale. Southwest Airlines encourages having fun and showing humor and enthusiasm at work. This is illustrated in their interview process, which includes group interviews where applicants tell jokes and role-play a variety of situations to demonstrate teamwork, a sense of humor, and the capacity to act spontaneously.

Some conscious businesses place their employees in self-managing work teams. This allows each employee and team to have autonomy and some self-governing duties. This autonomy and a sense of belonging results in low employee turnover and high employee morale. Conscious businesses consider employees as an extension of the company's deeper purpose, allowing them to delight customers and give them experiences that create value. By valuing a purpose-driven motive, these businesses not only create experiences for their employees but also make long-lasting impressions on their customers.

A valued experience to customers. Conscious businesses understand that giving a customer an experience rather than just a mere transaction impacts customer loyalty. Conscious businesses consider their customers to be the very best marketing tool that they have. Word of mouth is still the most impactful marketing tool, and in today's social media–fueled environment, where every customer has a platform to share their experience with millions of people, a positive customer experience is even more vital for the health of a business. Based on this premise, conscious businesses create emotional connections that go beyond the mechanistic transaction.

Southwest Airlines' employees activated the emotional connection with customers by giving them experiences that are based on not only humor but going above and beyond expectations to meet customers' needs. Some examples include driving customers back home after missing their flights, caring for a customer's pet when there were no other alternatives, and allowing a customer to stay at an employee's home while undergoing medical treatment.

Conscious businesses understand the importance of the employee effectively communicating the company's purpose through their interactions and genuine engagement with consumers. In his book *It's Not What You Sell, It's What You Stand For,* Roy Spence Jr. wrote, "When you begin to make a difference in the lives of your customers, the quality of the relationship you and your employees have with the customer changes. The relationship evolves from a transaction to a partnership characterized by gratitude, respect, and sometimes even joy. This new dynamic will fuel a level of passion and engagement in employees that gets reinforced by every positive interaction with a customer."[15]

---

15 Roy M. Spence Jr. and Haley Rushing, *It's Not What You Sell, It's What You Stand For: Why Every Extraordinary Business Is Driven by Purpose* (New York: Portfolio, 2011).

The cultivation of passionate employees leads to experiences that beget passionate and loyal customers. Because of this higher purpose, conscious businesses strive to create quality products and services. This oftentimes results in a loyal customer base and viral word of mouth and/or organic public relations via social media and positive online customer reviews.

Commitment to the silent stakeholder. Conscious businesses value the environment and understand that they need to advocate for the only silent stakeholder. They are conscious of how environmental challenges such as pollution and wasted energy sources impact the ecosystem and the well-being of humankind and are optimistic that their efforts will make an impact in making the world a better place for future generations.

Raj Sisodia, coauthor with John Mackey of *Conscious Capitalism: Liberating the Heroic Spirit of Business,* notes that implementing proenvironmental practices could benefit all stakeholders: "As a business becomes more energy efficient, it saves money; as a business reduces its waste, it spends less money on packaging and disposable products. Both are good for business, good for the environment, and good for all the other stakeholders."

Google is a conscious business, and it has a website, Google Green, that shares how they are aligning their services, products, and corporate environment with their commitment to a better environment. These efforts result in saving energy, reducing costs, and increasing efficiency.

Besides environmental stewardship, conscious businesses value involvement in humanitarian causes on both the local and global level. They recognize that they are connected to a larger world and have unconditional responsibilities that extend beyond the walls (physical or digital) of the company. Through volunteerism, donations, collaborations, and philanthropic foundations, conscious businesses value the act of making a difference in a positive way.

New Balance has 105 years of community outreach history that is woven into their company DNA. The New Balance Foundation, through donations and volunteerism, carries out their mission to support charitable organizations whose humanitarian efforts work for the betterment of our children and communities, with a principal focus on promoting healthy lifestyles while working toward the prevention of childhood obesity. In service of this mission, the Foundation supports grassroots children's initiatives in the communities in which New Balance operates facilities.

Timberland makes an impact in the world by advocating for social justice, protecting the outdoors, improving workers' lives, and engaging in community service. In addition to their environmental efforts, Google devised Google Earth Outreach, a collaboration with the Office of the United Nations High Commissioner for Refugees (UNHCR), to increase the visibility of some of the most remote areas of the world to help illustrate and maximize humanitarian efforts in areas of major crises and displacement.

Interconnected stakeholder groups. Conscious businesses value cooperation, connectedness, fairness, balance, and value creation. They understand that the cooperation between stakeholders is the essence of being able to communicate and attain the business's higher purpose.

When conflicts arise and compromises are needed, conscious businesses work to find solutions that go above the details of the conflict and harmonize the group based on their shared purpose and values. Through stakeholder relationships, conscious businesses value fairness, value creation, connectedness, and balance.

The ultimate result of Conscious Capitalism is social wellness. If the four tenets of Conscious Capitalism—Purpose, Stakeholder Orientation, Conscious Leadership, and Conscious Culture—can be the universal tenets of our economy, we will all benefit. Innovation, creativity, respect, and a higher purpose can fuel capitalism with a higher intensity than greed ever has. We as entrepreneurs, business owners, consumers, and investors can shift the economic system toward a better capitalistic system that we will all benefit from. The concept of Conscious Capitalism is well summed up in the established credo found on the website www.consciouscapitalism.org. It reads, "Free enterprise capitalism is the most powerful system for social cooperation and human progress ever conceived. It is one of the most compelling ideas we humans have ever had. But we can aspire to even more."

A month after our last session, I got a postcard at my office. On the front was a seagull with a french fry in its mouth, standing on a beach. I flipped the card over and read: "Hi doc, Hope all is well. I'm here on the water, somewhere off Rhode Island, working with a crew of entrepreneurs who are creating offshore wind turbines. They're bringing clean energy to surrounding areas. Tough work but by the time we're done here, a bunch of people will be less dependent on fossil fuels."

Now, I have a whole folder filled with his colorful postcards from California, Alaska, Texas, and other states. Each one makes me smile.

One of his latest was from Michigan, where Capitalism was hanging out with what he called his "fans," brainstorming with young restauranteurs on ways to use farm-to-table in new ways. He mentioned he was heading to Idaho next to meet with a business owner who was planning to give away all his wealth to important causes. It made me smile to see Capitalism sounding happier, working to make a difference.

I still see patients at my practice and still write in my journal afterward. I've also taken a page from Capitalism's book and joined a local mastermind of entrepreneurs with my wife. We go out for a date night after every meeting, chatting about the ways we can use my practice to make an even bigger difference in our community.

Life is good. It's different than it was a few years ago, and there are new challenges on the horizon, I'm sure. But I'm also aware many of us are working for a better world. With so many of us waking up, I'm optimistic about what the future has in store.

CHAPTER NINE

CONCLUSION

This book has detailed a hypothetical encounter with Capitalism as a patient on my couch. Now that I've explained my perspectives on how the psychological health (or dysfunction) of individuals has a direct link to the health of our economic system, let me clarify my views on capitalism. Capitalism is changing, not broken. Our relationship with capitalism is also shifting. Capitalism is a system just as delicate as the human psyche, and it requires the same care, nurturing, and purposeful engagement as each individual's psyche.

Capitalism, when based on social cooperation and collaborative growth, is arguably the most powerful social system conceived because it leverages people—and there is nothing more potent than the creativity, ingenuity, and innovation of people—as well as economic systems and social systems.

When any societal system, be it an individual or other system, is in dysfunction, it is commonly because the people in that system have a low level of social interest. Remember my patients Sue the workaholic manager and Brian the unhappy husband? They both had low levels of social interest, which negatively affected their lives on many levels.

An individual with a low level of social interest can be the weak link in a system. In capitalism, for example, people who are vulnerable to weaknesses within their own psyches and have potentially misguided goals and motivations may influence their communities and business as a whole.

Greed, one of the most common criticisms (incorrectly) levelled at capitalism, is actually a byproduct of egoism and self-centeredness, which are profound characteristics of low social interest. In other words, greed is a sign that something has gone amiss, not that the whole system is a problem. Greed leads to extreme, systematic dysfunction.

Individual challenges impact the system in many ways. For example, people with inaccurate views of capitalism may spread their views, leading to inconsistent interpretations of the intention of the system.

For example, business schools have consistently preached the conventional themes of maximizing shareholder value and competing against other stakeholders. Individual academics may have caused new generations to believe that business's sole purpose is to do whatever it takes to meet financial bottom lines, even to the detriment of others.

The roots of our misinterpretation are, in part, historic. For many years, capitalism was seen through an individualistic lens. Business owners pursued individual profit and did not acknowledge the impact their business or industry had on others. For example, a traditional economic view might see automobile manufacturing separately from mineral mining, petroleum production, and the workers on which those industries rely. Moreover, this view might also not acknowledge the impact that automobile manufacturing has on the environment, politics, and economic status of a community.

Fortunately, this is not the only view possible. Capitalism is a flexible and responsive social system that can evolve with our collective values and societal needs.

And our societal needs *have* changed, demanding evolution and change. Since capitalism was established as our economic system, we have endured significant societal changes that have altered not only our commercial operation but our viewpoints on commerce as a whole. We are now mindful of the untallied costs of the depletion of natural resources, workforce exploitation, sustained and growing wage gaps, corporate fraud, and the erosion of public trust in companies and their leadership. My own survey showed how individuals are aware of the consciousness of companies and how their perception can change over time, based on what companies do.

While our needs have changed and some individuals are becoming conscious (with businesses reacting, impacting the system as a whole), there remains an incongruity between the societal rise in consciousness and the way we are often taught to think about capitalism. And we must fix that.

Just as some psychotherapy methods aim to reframe and reeducate people on how they view their roles in life and increase their levels of social interest, we can reframe and reeducate ourselves on the way we approach capitalism, and redefine what our roles are within the greater economic/social system.

Getting Capitalism off the Couch

In my practice, when I have a patient, the goal is to provide them with the tools they need in the real world. Eventually, my patients work with me to address their concerns and get empowered with some new resources. There comes a time when they no longer need to visit.

Before a last meeting with a patient, we will review whether the patient can work on their own. We will discuss what they have learned and what they can do to move forward. My patient and I chat about their support systems. I usually ask my patient to self-report on whether they feel good and confident about moving forward without my support. It is only after all of this that the patient stops making their appointments and goes forth, armed with what they need to live their lives. Even then, my door is always open.

If capitalism were my patient, I would do the same. But, even more importantly, I think this process works for our relationship with capitalism. Together, you and I have discussed capitalism, reframing, and what has made individuals within capitalism dysfunctional.

Now we're ready to move forward together with a healthier relationship with capitalism. Let's take a look at this final process again, now that we have gone through a review of sorts at the start of this chapter.

Your Tools

Your tools, whether you are a consumer or business owner, are immense. If you're a customer, like those I spoke with in my survey, you have the chance to vote with your dollar. Keep your ear to the ground and uncover what you can about the company you do business with. Take advantage of the amazing tools at your disposal, including social media and the greater transparency companies have adhered to since the great collapse of 2008. Learn more about capitalism and make an effort to foster businesses doing good.

If you are a business owner, you can choose to change how you do business. If you've always focused on shareholders and profit, now is the time to zoom your focus outward and consider all the stakeholders your company impacts. What greater purpose could you serve and what real legacy could you leave to your employees, your customers, your community, and the world at large? How can you do business with vendors and suppliers who are like-minded and conscious?

Most of all, practice being a good and conscious member of our larger society, whether you are a business owner or customer. This may seem simplistic, but it is not. Awareness and conscious choice are a big part of therapy.

A while ago, a nurse practitioner came to me because she always felt upset and she had trouble relaxing. I gave her some homework: "Every day, for ten minutes, try relaxing."

"That's it?" she asked, sounding confused.

"That's it," I confirmed.

"But how? What if I do it wrong?"

"Just try. We can start by reviewing some ideas."

Once I got her talking, my patient had all kinds of ideas how she could relax—yoga, meditation, quiet music, sleeping, sitting still, going on a walk. She knew what to do, but somehow being given this task as homework allowed her to actually apply what she knew.

Reader, I give you the same homework: just try. You won't get it perfect, but you likely have some ideas on how to make the world a better place through your role in capitalism. Maybe you have already considered joining Conscious Capitalism, starting your own conscious business, or doing business only with companies whose ethics you admire. When you start taking these small steps, you notice that your relationship with capitalism and your relationship with yourself as a consumer or business owner starts to shift. That's the beauty of doing this type of work.

Self-Report

Take a look at your situation. Are you blaming capitalism for dysfunction? Are you ready to take responsibility for your own role in the system of capitalism? Are you willing to do the hard work of becoming a conscious consumer or conscious business?

Make time to check in with yourself. Consider journaling or reflecting on what your relationship with capitalism is and how it is changing. What is your own role, and how are the steps you are taking affecting your relationship to capitalism and to those around you? Keep track so you can see the trajectory of your journey.

What Are Your Support Systems?

Fortunately, if you want to harness the vast power of capitalism, there are support systems to help you. Conscious Capitalism is a worldwide movement and may have chapters near you, where you can learn more about the movement and get involved. In addition, the media and annual report of specific companies can help you evaluate which companies you want to support with your purchases and investments.

If you own a business, B lab is an organization that can help you find resources to get certified as a B Corporation. They also have resources to help business owners who want to make a difference. In addition, there are many books and masterminds that discuss how to start and run a conscious business.

Doing the Work on Your Own

It's not uncommon for a couple to come into my office and for one person to have already done my work for me. Sometimes, a partner comes in with a diagnosis, even though it's my name on the door: "The problem is that he doesn't listen." "The trouble is that he always nags." "She never helps around the house—that's the real issue."

By taking a patient history and by setting some goals, one of the things my patients usually learn is that both parties are involved in any relationship. Even if one party is convinced, it's the other person who's the "problem." In therapy, patients find both sides have a role to play in building a stronger relationship.

As you've read this book, you've likely noticed that this relationship we have with capitalism is like that. It began with capitalism on the couch, but over the course of the book it's become clear we all have a role to play in improving our relationship with this system. It's easy to point fingers, but in the therapist's office and in life, casting blame rarely gets results. Taking some responsibility for what you can do is what is needed. So while capitalism is working on itself through Conscious Capitalism, this is also an invitation to look within and to see how your own relationship with the community, the economy, and your personal relationships can be shifted so you are contributing in positive ways.

You're ready for this. You're ready to head out there with eyes open and to realize you're part of a powerful system and living during a time of rapid change. You can make smart changes that help to combat individual dysfunction, so your own contribution makes the capitalist systems stronger for everyone.

And, finally, my door is always open.

VIENNA

Belvedere Palace

Hey doc,
I'm staying near Hernalser Hauptstraße in Vienna's 17th district. These are Alfred Adler's stomping grounds when he was young. Thinking of you and knowing you're still out there, making a difference with business.

Upper Belvedere Prinz Eugen-Straße 27 – 1030 Vienna – Austria

BIBLIOGRAPHY

"2018 Tech Tour." Women Tech Council. http://www.womentechcouncil.com/programs
/student-innovators/2018-tech-tour/.

Aburdene, Patricia. *Megatrends 2010: The Rise of Conscious Capitalism*. Charlottes-
ville, VA: Hampton Roads Publishing, 2007.

Alsop, Ronald J. "Business Ethics Education in Business Schools: A Commentary."
Journal of Management Education 30, no. 1 (2006): 11–14.

"American Greed." CNBC. http://www.cnbc.com/id/18057119.

Andzulis, James, Nikolaos G. Panagopoulos, and Adam Rapp. "A Review of Social
Media and Implications for the Sales Process." *Journal of Personal Selling and Sales
Management* 3 (2012): 305–16.

Antony, Michael V. "Concepts of Consciousness, Kinds of Consciousness, Meanings
of 'Consciousness.'" *Philosophical Studies* 109, no. 1 (2002): 1–16.

Arnulf, Jan Ketil and Petter Gottschalk. "Heroic Leaders as White-Collar Criminals:
An Empirical Study." *Journal of Investigative Psychology and Offender Profiling* 10,
no. 1 (2012): 96–113.

Babbie, E. R. *The Basics of Social Research*. Belmont, CA: Wadsworth Publishing
Company, 2008.

Bainbridge, Stephen M. "In Defense of the Shareholder Wealth Maximization Norm:
A Reply to Professor Green." *Washington and Lee Law Review* 50, no. 4 (Fall 1993):
1423–47.

Banerjee, S. B. "Corporate Social Responsibility: The Good, the Bad and the Ugly."
Critical Sociology 34, no. 1 (2008): 51–79.

Barlas, S. "Obama Administration Establishes Corporate Fraud Task Force." *Strategic
Finance* 91, no. 7 (January 2010): 25.

Belluck, Pam. "Prosecutors Say Greed Drove Pharmacist to Dilute Drugs." *New York
Times*, August 18, 2001. https://www.nytimes.com/2001/08/18/us/prosecutors-say
-greed-drove-pharmacist-to-dilute-drugs.html.

Bemporad, R., and B. Mitch Baranowski. *Conscious Consumers Are Changing the
Rules of Marketing. Are You Ready? Highlights from the BBMG Conscious Consumer
Report*. BBMG, 2007.

"The Birth of the Web." CERN. http://home.web.cern.ch/about/birth-web.

Bjugstad, K., E. C. Thach, K. J. Thompson, and A. Morris. "A Fresh Look at Fol-lowership: A Model for Matching Followership and Leadership Styles." *Journal of Behavioral and Applied Management* 7, no. 3 (2006): 304–19.

Boddy, C. R. "The Corporate Psychopaths Theory of the Global Financial Crisis." *Journal of Business Ethics* 102, no. 2 (2011): 255–59.

Branden, N. *The Art of Living Consciously: The Power of Awareness to Transform Everyday Life*. New York: Fireside, 1999.

Bresser-Pereira, L. C. "Five Models of Capitalism." *Revista de Economia Política* 32, no. 1 (2012): 21–32.

Brown, A. "The New Follower-Ship: A Challenge for Leaders. *Futurist* 37, no. 2 (2003): 68.

Bruhn, J. G., and J. Lowrey. "The Good and Bad about Greed: How the Manifesta-tions of Greed Can Be Used to Improve Organizational and Individual Behavior and Performance." *Consulting Psychology Journal: Practice and Research* 64, no. 2 (2012): 136.

Burns, J. M. *Leadership*. New York: Harper & Row, 1978.

"Business Schools: Bad for Business?" *The Economist*, February 19, 2005.

Butcher, K., B. Sparks, and F. O'Callaghan. "Effect of Social Influence on Repurchase Intentions." *Journal of Services Marketing* 16, no. 6 (2002): 503–14.

Caesar, S. "Round Up." *Education for Primary Care* 20 (2009): 471–76.

Cavender, G., K. Gray, and K. W. Miller "Enron's Perp Walk: Status Degradation Cer-emonies as Narrative." *Crime, Media, Culture* 6, no. 3 (2010): 251–66.

Chapman, B. and Raj Sisodia. *Everybody Matters: The Extraordinary Power of Caring for Your People Like Family*. New York: Penguin Random House, 2015.

Chatterjee, P. "Online Reviews: Do Consumers Use Them?" *Advances in Consumer Research* 28 (2001): 129–33.

Clark Jr., W. H., and E. K. Babson. "How Benefit Corporations Are Redefining the Purpose of Business Corporations." *William Mitchell Law Review* 38 (2011): 817.

Conscious Capitalism. www.consciouscapitalism.org.

Crainer, S. "Purpose Special Report." *Business Strategy Review* 22, no. 3 (2011): 11–16.

Crandall, J. E. "A Scale for Social Interest." *Journal of Individual Psychology* 31, no. 2 (1975): 187–95.

Curran, K., K. O'Hara, and S. O'Brien. "The Role of Twitter in the World of Business." *International Journal of Business Data Communications and Networking* 7, no. 3 (2011): 1–15.

Damouni, Nadia. "Highest-Paid U.S. CEOs Are Often Fired or Fined—Study. *Reuters*, August 28, 2013. https://www.reuters.com/article/companies-pay/highest-paid-u-s-ceos-are-often-fired-or-fined-study-idUSL2N0GT0Y320130828.

Dobson, John. "Is Shareholder Wealth Maximization Immoral?" *Financial Analysts Journal* 55, no. 5 (1999): 69–75.

Dominelli, A. "Web Surveys-Benefits and Considerations." *Clinical Research and Regulatory Affairs* 20, no. 4 (2003): 409–16.

Donaldson, T., and L. E. Preston. "The Stakeholder Theory of the Corporation: Concepts, Evidence, and Implications." *Academy of Management Review* 20, no. 1 (1995): 65–91.

eBay. *Global Impact 2016 Summary.* https://static.ebayinc.com/assets/Uploads /Documents/eBay-Global-Impact-2016Summary.pdf.

Edosomwan, S., S. K. Prakasan, D. Kouame, J. Watson, and T. Seymour. "The History of Social Media and Its Impact on Business." *Journal of Applied Management and Entrepreneurship* 16, no. 3 (2011): 79–91.

Feuerberg, G. "Greed, Lack of Transparency Caused Financial Crisis, Says Greenberger." *The Epoch Times*, New York edition, November 8, 2012, A7.

Forbes, S. "Capitalism: A True Love Story." *Forbes Inc.* 184, no. 7 (2009): 24–28.

Freeman, E., L. Stewart, and B. Moriarty. "Teaching Business Ethics in the Age Of Madoff." *Change: The Magazine of Higher Learning* 41, no. 6 (2009): 37–42.

Freeman, E. R. *Strategic Management: A Stakeholder Approach.* Cambridge, MA: Ballinger, 1984.

Frey, Erin. "The New Frontier—Therapy in the Workplace." Medium, July 12, 2017. https:// medium.com/kip-blog/the-new-frontier-therapy-in-the-workplace-aadb91735628.

Friedman, D. *Morals and Markets: An Evolutionary Account of the Modern World.* New York: Palgrave Macmillan, 2008.

Friedman, H. H., and L. W. Friedman. "How Virtuous Is Your Firm? A Checklist." *Electronic Journal of Business Ethics and Organization Studies* 14, no. 1 (2009): 14–20.

Friedman, M. *Capitalism and Freedom.* With Rose D. Friedman. Chicago: University of Chicago Press, 1962.

Friedman, M. "The Social Responsibility of Business Is to Increase Its Profits." *New York Times Magazine*, September 13, 1970, 122–26.

Friedrichs, David. "Enron Et Al.: Paradigmatic White Collar Crime Cases for the New Century." *Critical Criminology* 12, no. 2 (2004): 113–32.

Frohnen, B., and L. Clarke. "Scandal in Corporate America: An Ethical, Not a Legal Problem." *USA Today*, November 2002, 131, 24–26.

Fry, L. W. and J. Slocum. "Maximizing the Triple Bottom Line through Spiritual Leadership." *Organizational Dynamics* 37, no. 1 (2008): 86–96.

Gerzema, J. and M. D'Antonio. *The Athena Doctrine: How Women (and the Men Who Think Like Them) Will Rule the Future.* San Francisco: Young & Rubicam, 2013.

Given, L. M. (ed). *The SAGE Encyclopedia of Qualitative Research Methods.* Vol. 2. Thousand Oaks, CA: Sage Publications, 2008.

Goodin, R. E. "Choose Your Capitalism?" *Comparative European Politics* 1, no. 2 (2003): 203–13.

"Greed." *Oxford Learners Dictionaries.* https://www.oxfordlearnersdictionaries.com /definition/english/greed?q=greed.

Greenberg, M. "Do Americans Still Care about the Environment?" *The Environment Systems and Decisions* 23, no. 4 (2003): 283–84.

Greenhouse, S. "How Costco Became the Anti-Wal-Mart." *New York Times*, July 17, 2005, https://www.nytimes.com/2005/07/17/business/yourmoney/how-costco-became -the-antiwalmart.html.

Hanna, R., A. Rohm, and V. L. Crittenden. "We're All Connected: The Power of the Social Media Ecosystem." *Business Horizons* 54, no. 3 (2011): 265–73.

Haque, Umair. *The New Capitalist Manifesto: Building a Disruptively Better Business.* Boston: Harvard Business Press, 2011.

Harrison, P. "Adam Smith and the History of the Invisible Hand." *Journal of the History of Ideas* 72, no. 1 (2011): 29–49.

Hinkin, T. R., and J. B. Tracey. "What Makes It So Great? An Analysis of Human Resources Practices Among Fortune's Best Companies to Work For." *Cornell Hospitality Quarterly* 51, no. 2 (2010): 158–70.

Holbrook, E. "Rise of the B Corp." *Risk Management* 57, no. 7 (2010): 12.

Hoseong, J. and C. Beomjoon. "The Relationship between Employee Satisfaction and Customer Satisfaction." *Journal of Services Marketing* 26, no. 5 (2012): 332–41.

James Jr, H. S. and F. Rassekh. "Smith, Friedman, and Self-Interest in Ethical Society." *Business Ethics Quarterly* 10, no. 3 (July 2000): 659–74.

Johnson, Craig. E. *Meeting the Ethical Challenges of Leadership: Casting Light or Shadow.* Thousand Oaks, CA: Sage Publications, 2011.

Jordi, C. L. "Rethinking the Firm's Mission and Purpose." *European Management Review* 7, no. 4 (2010): 195–204.

Karns, G. L. "Stewardship: a New Vision for the Purpose of Business." *Corporate Governance* 11, no. 4 (2011): 337–47.

Kaufman, H. "What Would Adam Smith Say Now?" *Business Economics* 36, no. 4 (2001): 7–12.

Keane, M. T., M. O'Brien, and B. Smyth. "Are People Biased in Their Use of Search Engines?" *Communications of the ACM* 51, no. 2 (2008): 49–52.

Kiesler, S., J. Siegel, and T. W. McGuire. "Social Psychological Aspects of Computer-Mediated Communication." *American Psychologist* 39, no. 10 (1984): 11–23.

Kietzmann, J. H., K. Hermkens, I. P. McCarthy, and B. S. Silvestre. "Social Media? Get Serious! Understanding the Functional Building Blocks of Social Media." *Business Horizons* 54, no. 3 (2011): 241–51.

Kirtiş, A. K., and F. Karahan. "To Be or Not to Be in Social Media Arena as the Most Cost-Efficient Marketing Strategy After the Global Recession." *Procedia-Social and Behavioral Sciences* 24 (2011): 260–68.

Kitchen, P. J., and D. E. Schultz. *Raising the Corporate Umbrella: Corporate Communication in the 21st Century.* Basingstoke, UK: Palgrave Macmillan, 2001.

Kofman, F. *Conscious Business: How to Build Value through Values.* Louisville, CO: Sounds True, 2006.

Kohn, A. *No Contest: The Case Against Competition.* Wilmington, MA: Mariner Books, 1992.

Koys, D. J. "The Effects of Employee Satisfaction, Organizational Citizenship Behavior, and Turnover on Organizational Effectiveness: A Unit-Level, Longitudinal Study." *Personnel Psychology* 54, no. 1 (2001): 101–14.

Kramer, R. M. "Rethinking Trust." *Harvard Business Review* 87, no. 6 (2009): 69–77.

Krugman, Paul. "How Did Economists Get It So Wrong?" *New York Times*, September 2, 2009. https://www.nytimes.com/2009/09/06/magazine/06Economic-t.html.

Lachman, M. E. "Aging Under Control." *Psychological Science Agenda*, January 19, 2005. https://www.apa.org/science/about/psa/2005/01/lachman.

Laroche, M., J. Bergeron, and G. Barbaro-Forleo. "Targeting Consumers Who Are Willing to Pay More for Environmentally Friendly Products." *Journal of Consumer Marketing* 18, no. 6 (2001): 503–20.

Lebowitz, M. A. "What Keeps Capitalism Going?" *Monthly Review* 56, no. 2 (2004). https://monthlyreview.org/2004/06/01/what-keeps-capitalism-going/.

Legault, Marie. "Conscious Capitalism: Leaders and Organizations with a World View." *Integral Leadership Review*, March 2012. http://integralleadershipreview.com/6686-conscious-capitalism-leaders-and-organizations-with-a-world-view/.

Loderer, C. and L. Roth, U. Waelchli, and P. Joerg. "Shareholder Value: Principles, Declarations, and Actions." *Financial Management* 39, no. 1 (2010): 5–32.

Lowney, C. *Heroic Leadership: Best Practices from a 450-Year-Old Company That Changed the World.* Chicago: Loyola Press, 2003.

Löwy, M. "Marx and Weber: Critics of Capitalism." *New Politics* 11, no. 2 (2007): 146–52

Lux, K. "The Failure of the Profit Motive." *Ecological Economics* 44, no. 1 (2003): 1–9.

Mackey, J. "Creating a New Paradigm for Business." In *Be the Solution*, edited by M. Strong, 73–113. Hoboken, NJ: John Wiley & Sons, 2009.

Mackey, J. "What Conscious Capitalism Really Is: A Response to James O'Toole and David Vogel's 'Two and a Half Cheers for Conscious Capitalism.'" *California Management Review* 53, no. 3 (2011): 83–90.

Mackey, J. and Raj Sisodia. *Conscious Capitalism: Liberating the Heroic Spirit of Business.* Boston: Harvard Business School Publishing, 2013.

Maitland, I. "The Human Face of Self-Interest." *Journal of Business Ethics* 38, nos. 1–2 (2002): 3–17.

Mangold, W. G. and D. J. Faulds. "Social Media: The New Hybrid Element of the Promotion Mix." *Business Horizons* 52, no. 4 (2009): 357–65.

Marconi, J. *Future Marketing: Targeting Seniors, Boomers, and Generation X and Y.* Lincolnwood, IL: NTC Business Books, 2001.

McMillan, D. W., and D. M. Chavis. "Sense of Community: A Definition and Theory." *Journal of Community Psychology* 14, no. 1 (1986): 6–23.

Meyer, H. "When the Cause Is Just." *Journal of Business Strategy* 20, no. 6 (1999): 27–31.

Meyers, D. G. "COMMENTARIES: Costs and Benefits of American Corporate Capitalism." *Psychological Inquiry* 18, no. 1 (2007): 43–47.

Molenaar, C. *E-Marketing: Applications of Information Technology and the Internet within Marketing.* Abington, UK: Routledge, 2011.

Mourkogiannis, N. "On Purpose." *Business Strategy Review* 18, no. 1 (2007): 38–41.

Murray, Sara. "Benefit Corporations: Companies Obliged to Do Good." *Financial Times,* April 23, 2012.

Naughton, K. "The CEO Party Is Over." *Newsweek,* December 29, 2002. https://www.newsweek.com/ceo-party-over-141319.

O'Toole, J. and D. Vogel. "Two and a Half Cheers for Conscious Capitalism." *California Management Review* 53, no. 3 (2011): 60–76.

Omran, M., P. Atrill, and J. Pointon. "Shareholders versus Stakeholders: Corporate Mission Statements and Investor Returns." *Business Ethics: A European Review* 11, no. 4 (2002): 318–26.

Onwuegbuzie, A. J. and R. B. Johnson. "The Validity Issue in Mixed Research." *Research in the Schools* 13, no. 1 (2006): 48–63.

Pearson, K. "Whole Foods Market™ Case Study: Leadership and Employee Retention." Johnson & Wales University, Providence, RI, 2012.

Peck, Emily. "This Small Company Offers On-Site Therapy to Workers." *Huffington Post,* January 12, 2016. https://www.huffpost.com/entry/certified-angus-beef-therapy_n_56707e76e4b011b83a6d0755.

Percy, D. "Increasingly Rapid Turnover to Become Norm." *Saskatoon Star-Phoenix,* May 27, 2006. http://search.proquest.com.ezproxy.apollolibrary.com/docview/348774620?accountid=458.

Peruta, A., W. Ryan, and G. Acquavella. "Organizational Approaches to Social Media Branding: Comparing Brand Facebook Pages and Web Sites." International Conference on Communication, Media, Technology and Design, 2012.

Phillips, R., R. E. Freeman, and A. C. Wicks. "What Stakeholder Theory Is Not." *Business Ethics Quarterly* 13, no. 4 (2003): 479–502.

Pliska, R. J. "Social Media: Identifying the Business Opportunities, the Personal Experiences of a Social Media User." *Real Estate Issues* 37, no. 1 (2012): 48.

Rand, A., N. Branden, A. Greenspan, and R. Hessen. *Capitalism: the Unknown Ideal.* New York: New American Library, 1967.

Rand, A., N. Branden, A. Greenspan, and R. Hessen. *What Is Capitalism?* Wilmington, DE: Second Renaissance Book Service, 1967.

"Recommendations from Friends Remain Most Credible Form of Advertising Among Consumers; Branded Websites Are the Second-Highest-Rated Form." Nielsen, September 28, 2015. https://www.nielsen.com/eu/en/press-releases/2015/recommendations-from-friends-remain-most-credible-form-of-advertising/.

Reed, Jennifer. "A New Business Model." *Success,* September 5, 2011. https://www.success.com/a-new-business-model/.

Romano, R. "The Sarbanes-Oxley Act and the Making of Quack Corporate Governance." *The Yale Law Journal* 114 (2005): 1521–1611. https://pdfs.semanticscholar.org/5605/89dfbc9d6b7a7b1be31df7f5c28fd8428892.pdf.

Rost, J. C. "Leadership Development in the New Millennium." *Journal of Leadership & Organizational Studies* 1, no. 1 (1993): 91–110.

Ryan, Jason. "Fraud 'Directly Related' to Financial Crisis Probed." *ABC News*, February 11, 2009.

Schwerin, D. A. "Globally-Conscious Capitalism: A Conscious Perspective on Economic Management and Responsibility." *Frontier Perspectives* 13, no. 2 (Fall/Winter 2004): 46–49.

Selby, Sharon. "Anxiety Viewed through a Different Lens . . . From Adlerian Theory." Sharon Selby, March 8, 2015. https://www.sharonselby.com/parenting/viewing-anxiety-different-lens-adlerian-theory.

Sendjaya, S. and J. C. Sarros. "Servant Leadership: Its Origin, Development, and Application in Organizations. *Journal of Leadership & Organizational Studies* 9, no. 2 (2002): 57–64.

Sisodia, Raj. "Doing Business in the Age of Conscious Capitalism." *Journal of Indian Business Research* 1, nos. 2–3 (2009): 188–92.

Sisodia, Raj. "Conscious Capitalism: A Better Way to Win: A Response to James O'Toole and David Vogel's 'Two and a Half Cheers for Conscious Capitalism.'" *California Management Review* 53, no. 3 (2011): 98–108.

Sisodia, Raj, D. B. Wolfe, and J. N. Shet. *Firms Of Endearment: How World-Class Companies Profit from Passion and Purpose.* Upper Saddle River, NJ: Wharton School Publishing, 2007.

Skeel, D. "The Empty Legacy of the Corporate Scandals." *Challenge* 48, no. 1 (2005): 104–17.

Smircich, Linda. "Concepts of Culture and Organizational Analysis." *Administrative Science Quarterly* 28, no. 3 (1983): 339–58.

Smith, A. *The Wealth of Nations.* Edited by Charles J. Bullock. New York: Cosimo Classics, 2007.

Spence, R. *It's Not What You Sell, It's What You Stand For: Why Every Extraordinary Business Is Driven by Purpose.* New York: Penguin Random House, 2009.

Strong, M. (ed.) *Be the Solution: How Entrepreneurs and Conscious Capitalists Can Solve All the World's Problems.* Hoboken, NJ: John Wiley & Sons, 2009.

Thomas, L. M. "Sending Marketing Messages within Social Media Networks." *Journal of Internet Law* 14, no. 1 (2010): 3–4.

Thorne, B. M., and J. M. Giesen. *Statistics for the Behavioral Sciences.* Mayfield Mountain View, CA: McGraw-Hill Education, 2002.

Tindell, K. *Uncontainable: How Passion, Commitment, and Conscious Capitalism Built a Business Where Everyone Thrives.* New York: Grand Central Publishing, 2014.

Todd, Z., B. Nerlich, S. McKeown, and D. Clarke (eds.). *Mixing Methods in Psychology: The Integration of Qualitative and Quantitative Methods in Theory and Practice.* New York: Psychology Press, 2005.

Vagts, D. F. "Financial Meltdown and Its International Implications." *The American Journal of International Law* 103 (2009): 684.

Vallance, E. "What Is Business For? Ethics and the Aim of Business." *Business Strategy Review* 4, no. 1 (1993): 45–52.

Ver Eecke, W. "Adam Smith and the Free Market." In *Ethical Reflections on the Financial Crisis 2007/2008,* 5–21. New York, NY: Springer-Verlag Berlin Heidelberg, 2013.

Verschoor, C. "Are the Rich More Unethical and Greedy?" *Strategic Finance* 93, no. 11 (2012): 15–17.

Vieten, C., T. Amorok, and M. M. Schlitz. "I to We: The Role of Consciousness Transformation in Compassion and Altruism." *Zygon®* 41, no. 4 (2006): 915–32.

Vinod, S., and B. Sudhakar. "Servant Leadership: A Unique Art of Leadership." *Interdisciplinary Journal of Contemporary Research in Business* 2, no. 11 (2011): 456.

Waddock, S., and M. McIntosh. "Business Unusual: Corporate Responsibility in a 2.0 World*." *Business and Society Review* 116, no. 3 (2011): 303–30.

Wagner, S., and L. Dittmar. "The Unexpected Benefits of Sarbanes-Oxley." *Harvard Business Review* 84, no. 4 (2006): 133.

Wang, L., D. Malhotra, and J. K. Murnighan. "Economics Education and Greed." *Academy of Management Learning & Education* 10, no. 4 (2011): 643–60.

Wang, L., and J. K. Murnighan. "On Greed." *The Academy of Management Annals* 5, no. 1 (2011): 279–316.

Wargo, D. T., N. Baglini, and K. Nelson. "The Global Financial Crisis—Caused by Greed, Moral Meltdown and Public Policy Disasters." Forum on Public Policy, 2009.

Weber, Larry. *Marketing to the Social Web: How Digital Customer Communities Build Your Business.* Hoboken, NJ: John Wiley & Sons, 2009.

Webster Jr, Frederick. E. "Determining the Characteristics of the Socially Conscious Consumer." *Journal of Consumer Research* 2, no. 3 (December 1975): 188–96.

Windsor, D. "Shareholder Wealth Maximization." In *Finance Ethics: Critical Issues in Theory and Practice,* edited by J. R. Boatright, 435–55. Hoboken, NJ: John Wiley & Sons, 2011.

Yunus, Muhammad. "Social Business Entrepreneurs are the Solution." In *Humanism in Business,* edited by Heiko Spitzeck, Wolfgang Amann, Michael Pirson, Shiban Khan, and Ernst von Kimakowitz, 402–12. New York: Cambridge University Press, 2009.

Zakaria, F. "The Capitalist Manifesto: Greed Is Good." *Newsweek,* June 12, 2009.

Dr. Glen F. Pastores is an organization development consultant and coach, licensed marriage and family therapist, professor of psychology, and a Conscious Capitalist. He has held clinical, educational, and leadership positions in the psychology field. After completing a BA degree in psychology at San Diego State University and an MA in counseling psychology at National University, he obtained a PsyD in organization development at Alliant International University—California School of Professional Psychology. He has been providing psychotherapy services for more than twenty years, teaches psychology courses to undergraduate and graduate students, and has been a business consultant and executive coach for the past ten years.

Obtaining a PsyD degree in organization development (OD) helped Dr. Pastores learn how to manage change in organizational systems and how to work with individuals within a social context. It also sparked a life-long interest in the application of psychology and social justice in organizational systems, a subject discovered as part of a passion board project in his doctoral program and as part of his dissertation on Conscious Capitalism and conscious business practices.

Influenced by the work of Alfred Adler and his own experience in the field, Dr. Pastores believes that businesses have a higher purpose beyond profit, and that people have a desire to strive toward significance in their lives and to pursue an interest in contributing to their own communities and to human flourishing as a whole. This book blends these two beliefs of psychology and organization development together.

Dr. Pastores is a clinical fellow of the American Association of Marriage and Family Therapists, a clinical member of the California Association of Marriage and Family Therapists, and a member of the Asian American

Psychological Association. He is also a thought leader for Conscious Capitalism San Diego and one of the first psychotherapists to speak and write extensively about the connection between psychotherapy, human psychology, and business. Dr. Pastores also maintains a private psychotherapy practice and a consultation and executive coaching practice in San Diego, CA.

If you're curious about Dr. Pastores's research, which inspired this book, go to https://search.proquest.com/docview/1492730962/. For more information about his psychotherapy practice, visit www.glenfpastores.com. To learn more about his executive coaching and consultation practice, please visit www.drglenfpastores.com.

ELEVATE HUMANITY THROUGH BUSINESS.

Conscious Capitalism, Inc., supports a global community of business leaders dedicated to elevating humanity through business via their demonstration of purpose beyond profit, the cultivation of conscious leadership and culture throughout their entire ecosystem, and their focus on long-termism by prioritizing stakeholder orientation instead of shareholder primacy. We provide mid-market executives with innovative learning exchanges, transformational storytelling training, and inspiring conference experiences all designed to level-up their business operations and collectively demonstrate capitalism as a powerful force for good when practiced consciously.

We invite you, either as an individual or as a business, to join us and contribute your voice. Learn more about the global movement at www.consciouscapitalism.org.